Systems
Ethical Tools for **Change**

Information Systems Series
Series Editor: Professor I.O. Angell

Computer Security Within Organizations
Adrian R. Warman

Developing Information Systems
Concepts, Issues and Practice
Chrisanthi Avgerou and Tony Cornford

Effective Systems Design and Requirements Analysis
The ETHICS Approach
Enid Mumford

General Systems Theory
An Introduction
Lars Skyttner

Information in Action
Soft Systems Methodology
Lynda Davies and Paul Ledington

Information Systems Management
Opportunities and Risks
Ian O. Angell and Steve Smithson

Ourselves and Computers
Difference in Minds and Machines
Aart Bijl

Systems Design
Ethical Tools for Ethical Change
Enid Mumford

Understanding Information
An Introduction
Jonathan Liebenau and James Backhouse

Systems Design
Ethical Tools for Ethical Change

Enid Mumford

MACMILLAN

First published 1996 by
MACMILLAN PRESS LTD
Houndmills, Basingstoke, Hampshire RG21 6XS
and London
Companies and representatives
throughout the world

ISBN 0–333–66946–0

A catalogue record for this book is available
from the British Library.

10   9   8   7   6   5   4   3   2   1
05 04 03 02 01 00 99 98 97 96

Printed in Great Britain by
Antony Rowe Ltd, Chippenham, Wiltshire

Contents

Preface

This book is about making choices that take account of the needs and interests of a particular group of people, namely the employees of companies. The 'choice' situation that is discussed is when firms are making system changes, particularly changes that include technology. The author hopes that interested readers of the book will include systems designers, and other change agents, whose decisions can influence what is changed and how it is changed.

When major change is being introduced by a company there are usually a number of stakeholders. These include the shareholders who hope for increased profits, the senior managers who hope for performance awards and promotion, the customers who hope for better and cheaper products, the suppliers who hope that their business will increase as the company prospers and the employees who have to suffer the changes. At present the interests of shareholders, senior managers, customers and suppliers seem to be reasonably well taken care of, through increased dividends, performance-related pay, cost reductions and increased orders. The group that is less fortunate and, indeed, sometimes placed in a victim role, is the lower level management and non-managerial employees. They are experiencing loss of employment, greater insecurity and a deterioration in working conditions through longer hours, tighter controls and greater stress. The traditional friends of these employees seem no longer able to operate in a protective role. Trades unions have been seriously weakened by government policies, and the traditional personnel manager, who often mediated the boundary between employee and senior management interests, has changed into a bottom-line focused human resources manager.

American business books tell us that we live in volatile and uncertain times. To survive, companies must drastically restructure so that they become flatter and more flexible. One of the buzz phrases for this reorganization is business process re-engineering. The books also tell us that this volatile change process will continue indefinitely. But this is a hypothesis, and it remains to be seen whether it will prove to be correct. Biology suggests that continual change is unusual in nature. Most species develop through long periods of stability, interrupted by short periods of change.

The theory behind this book is that rapid change is usually followed by stability, and businesses and their employees both profit from this. Although change must be managed effectively, at the same time it is important to have strategies in place that encourage stability.

A great deal of what is happening in industry today would have been regarded as undesirable and unethical twenty years ago. Many of the UK's best companies, for example, Cadbury's, Lever Brothers and Bibby's, had Quaker owners and prided themselves on the security and good working conditions that they could offer their staff. They looked after their employees, with Cadbury's and Lever Brothers even providing their staff with high quality housing on attractive estates. They respected trades unions and were able to work with them on an amicable basis. They were successful companies that maintained their stability even when faced with major change.

This book presents a different hypothesis to the American one of continuous and chaotic change to which firms must respond or they will perish. It suggests that we will soon see some countervailing forces exerting an influence on company policies. One of these will be the labour market which, in Britain, has always been short of specialist skills. Firms will start competing for the increasing amount of skilled labour they require as technology advances and, to secure this, they will offer contracts and conditions of work that employees see as attractive.

A second countervailing force is likely to be the re-emergence of the trades unions in a new form. Like the German trades unions, they will be happy to collaborate with management in working hard for commercial success, but at the same time they will require employers to provide their members with job security and a good quality of working life. A new industrial relations climate will then cause ethical policies, practice and behaviour to become of renewed importance. Many companies wish to behave ethically and to provide job satisfaction and a good quality of working life for all their employees. This objective can be assisted by the kinds of decisions that are taken when change is introduced.

Taking an ethical position is never easy and everyone has to decide for themselves what is right or wrong, act in accordance with their decisions and accept the consequences of their conduct. Often there are moral dilemmas to be faced and a choice has to be made between a number of moral principles that may seem equally important. The two moral principles that most influence this book are ones that the author regards as important and, over the years, has been trying to contribute to in her own work. They are *quality of working life* and *freedom in work*. Quality of working life encompasses good working conditions, job security, opportunities for learning and personal development and adequate financial and other rewards. They are material things that the good company will provide. Freedom in work is the opportunity to exert influence, take decisions, make choices and to be regarded as a partner rather than as a subordinate.

The author has chosen to focus on how systems designers, and change agents, can assist the creation of this quality of working life and freedom because their roles as innovators place them in an influential position. The ethical position they take can have a major influence on the work experience of others. She also believes that in today's business world the interests of all stakeholders can be facilitated by the provision of these ethical conditions. Today's companies need creative, responsible employees able to solve problems, make choices and implement decisions. This is also what the modern worker and manager wants and so the interests of business and staff increasingly coincide. The introduction of technology provides particular opportunities for making ethical choices, as it can degrade or enhance the quality of working life, depending on the design route that is selected. It also presents new problems, the consequences of which cannot always be foreseen.

Computer professionals and other change agents have considerable power over the quality of working life and the freedom of other employees. The ethical position that they take can have a major impact on the work experience of others.

1 The past and the present

This chapter provides a brief historical account of the development of the factory system, the invention of new machines and the introduction and use of techniques associated with systems analysis and design. It sets the scene for our discussion of 'ethical' change: the kind of change that takes account of the needs of people.

The development of industry

For many years past most western industrial countries have been in the grip of a powerful ideology that is only now beginning to lose its force. This ideology has seen labour as an expendable, easily replaceable commodity which produces at highest efficiency and lowest cost when few demands are made of it, when work is tightly controlled and when little or no discretion is given to the individual. This philosophy arrived with the factory system and its need for organization and order. In 1776 Adam Smith, the Scottish political economist and philosopher, told the new British industrialists that they would increase efficiency and reduce costs by dividing the work process up into a large number of very simple tasks each one to be undertaken by a single worker [1]. Smith was clever enough to appreciate the consequences of this. He wrote in the *Wealth of Nations* that with this division of labour the worker would become:

> as stupid and ignorant as it is possible for a human creature to become ... his dexterity in his own particular trade, seems, in this manner to be acquired at the expense of his intellectual, social and martial virtues [2].

The wealthy classes were quite happy with this situation. They feared an educated workforce and were happy for poverty, work and education, or the lack of it, to be intertwined. Workers now became almost invisible. Their principal role was as sources of motive power, using their bodies and chiefly their hands and arms for this purpose [3].

Prior to the arrival of the factory system nine-tenths of English workers were peasants. Their conditions of life and work were very harsh but were somewhat softened by the religious doctrine of the time which maintained that men were born into particular stations of life. Along with this belief went an acceptance by the rich that they had a set of obligations to the poor. Also, the commercial dealings of the time were based on personal contact and so trust and esteem had high importance and the individual could not be separated from his economic interests [4]. These interests were always tempered by the social obligations that were a feature of medieval society.

1

Manufacturing, after the industrial revolution, required major capital investment and the employment of paid labour. Increased scale, although the most obvious, was not the most significant change. There was now a new social structure for production. For this to be profitable space and time had to be regulated. The clock, although invented in the thirteenth century, now had an important function – the regulation of timekeeping. This, in turn, had an effect on living quarters. Houses had to be close enough for the workforce to arrive at the specified time.

A philosopher and economist, Jeremy Bentham, a contemporary of Adam Smith, was greatly influenced by him and saw increasing material benefits as leading to greater happiness. Bentham was a liberal 'utilitarian' and believed that the rightness or wrongness of actions was determined by their consequences. He wanted to try to establish morals as an exact science and to subject it to rational thinking. Whereas the later work of Frederick Taylor was based on *l'homme boeuf*, the strong man who could be assisted to use his strength to maximise his material prosperity, Bentham was influenced by *l'homme machine*, the man who, once scientists understood why and how he reacted, could be made to perform in ways that assisted industrial production. In this way Bentham created the basis for economic planning and social engineering. Bentham saw the individual as being wholly egoistic, seeking pleasure and avoiding pain. Morality was the act of being happy and the principle of utility was to approve or disapprove of every action according to its ability to increase or diminish human happiness [5].

For Bentham, wealth was good because so much wealth produced an equivalent amount of happiness. Similarly, the happiness of a community was a product of economic sufficiency for its members. If the interests of society ever came into conflict with the interests of the individual then the two sets of interests must be brought into harmony through legislation. Legislation was Bentham's instrument for turning society into a predictable, well-ordered economic system.

This doctrine, called 'rationalism' was made explicit in the writings of eighteenth century philosophers and economists. It was based on a belief in human development and progress in which greater knowledge could lead to greater happiness. These ideas were given practical form by the engineering innovators of the time. In 1787, two years before Bentham published his book *An Introduction to the principles of morals and legislation*, James Watt produced his steam engine. This was the first attempt to apply technological principles concerning heat and mechanical energy to large-scale work problems. In doing this Watt bridged the gap between theoretical ideas and man's practical struggle to control his environment.

The technical developments of the time therefore reinforced and gave practical form to the new philosophical ideas of economic efficiency. By the beginning of the nineteenth century, in manufacturing processes like spinning and weaving, the problems of mechanical automation had been largely solved [6]. Given a large enough source of power, these machines could carry out every part of the process with no help from human hands other than tying threads together or identifying and correcting machine problems.

During the nineteenth century philosophy and technology continued to reinforce each other and the rigid division of labour continued to be accepted as an excellent form of industrial organization. In 1835, Charles Babbage, technologist and mathematician wrote:

> The constant repetition of the same process necessarily produces in the workman a degree of excellence and rapidity in his particular department, which is never possessed by a person who is obliged to execute many different processes.
>
> This rapidity is still further increased from the circumstances that most of the operations in factories where the division of labour is carried to a considerable extent, are paid for as piece work... [7].

These ideas did not go unchallenged. Karl Marx was now writing of the exploitation of the worker in the factory and of how he was deprived of culture and of the opportunity to become a complete man. Marx, like Bentham, believed in a rational social order, but one of a different kind from that he saw developing in Britain.

As industry developed, so economics became separated from ethics and utility from morality, and employment relationships became increasingly contractual. During the latter part of the second half of the nineteenth century the process of rationalization and mechanization began to speed up and this period saw the beginning of mass production industry and the fragmentation and deskilling of work previously performed by craftsmen. It also saw the appearance, in the United States, of the scientific management movement. The industrial philosophy of the time became to produce more things faster and the factory was seen as similar to a military establishment requiring both hierarchy and discipline [8]. However, this increased production was a result of more advanced machinery rather than mass demand and the entrepreneurs of the time had to create a market in order to justify the heavy capital investment that automatic machines required [9].

Frederick Winslow Taylor and his friend Frank Gilbreth, two pioneers of scientific management in the early years of the twentieth century, were greatly influenced by the ideas of Babbage. But, whereas Babbage had been a professor of mathematics at Cambridge, Taylor and Gilbreth were a practising engineer and a building contractor, respectively, and in an excellent position to apply their ideas.

Taylor's intention was very much in accord with the earlier philosophy of Bentham. Through applying intelligence and scientific method to what he saw as the muddle and inefficiency of industry, he proposed to increase the profitability of the enterprise and the earnings of employees. In this way both managers and workers would gain and conflict would change to harmony. This improvement was to be achieved by separating 'doing' from 'thinking' and allocating the first to workers and the second to management. The role of management was to study scientifically the best methods for carrying out tasks and for measuring the level of performance reached. The role of the worker was to obey [10].

The stopwatch was Taylor's tool for change. Before Taylor work had been timed, but only for the entire job. What Taylor did was to split each job into its component operations and take the time of each. This became the essence of scientific management: the systematic analysis and breakdown of work into the smallest combination and the rearrangement of the elements into the most efficient combination. Taylor's fame reached its height in 1899 when he taught a Dutchman named Schmidt to shovel forty-seven, instead of twelve and a half, tons of pig iron in the same time. He wrote, 'one of the very first requirements for a man who is fit to handle pig iron as a regular occupation is that he shall be so stupid and phlegmatic that he more nearly resemble an ox than any other type.' The unfortunate Schmidt did not appear to fit this description for we are told that while working for the Bethlehem Steel Company he was building his own house.

Taylor's principles reached their peak in 1914 when Henry Ford established a car assembly line at Highland Park, Michigan. The principle of machine-paced work which this embodied has led to the physical subordination of many workers, usually women, ever since. Even in today's computer age, the ability of technology to monitor and record the speed at which human beings work is still with us, and still used.

The scientific management movement was associated with a number of ideas and values. First, there was the belief that the human being could be treated as an operating unit to be adjusted by training and incentives to meet the needs of the organization. Second, there was the view that people were unreliable, with narrow capabilities and limited usefulness, and this justified their being given small, low discretion jobs. Third, labour was a commodity to be bought and sold by the organization and fourth, a materialistic ethic suggested that if the end of increased material comfort was achieved then this justified the means used to achieve it [11].

Like the nineteenth century, the twentieth century has had its critics of the rational ethic. They see today's society as dominated by technology and by technocratic power. Certainly, today's unemployment appears to be exacerbated by technical progress and by an urge to cut costs, with many large organizations increasing the size of their business as they reduce the numbers in their labour force.

During the 1970s Daniel Bell forecast the following changes. The economic sector would change from a goods-producing to a service economy. The technical and professional classes would dominate in occupational distribution. Knowledge would increase in importance and become the central factor in innovation and policy formulation. There would be greater control of technology and better technological assessment; and there would be the creation of a new intellectual technology to aid decision tasking. These predictions from twenty years ago seem to fit the present situation reasonably well [12]. They have been confirmed by Peter Drucker who tells us that by the end of the century 'knowledge workers' will make up a third or more of the workforce in the United States [13].

The development of computer technology

In England scientific progress took a step forward when, in November 1660, a group of men gathered together in Gresham College, London to hear a lecture. After this meeting they talked informally and it was suggested that a new College should be founded to promote Physico-Mathematical Experimental Learning and also to enable them to meet regularly. This was the start of the Royal Society – a British body which today rewards major scientific prowess in science and engineering by awarding the letters FRS – Fellow of the Royal Society. Other than the Nobel prize, this is the highest award a British scientist or engineer can receive.

At about the same time the first small step towards today's sophisticated computer technology was taken by a Frenchman, Blaise Pascal. He created the world's first calculating machine: a mechanical adder based on rotating cogs and wheels. Pascal was followed by a German, Gottfried Leibnitz, who produced a wheel which could multiply and perform calculations at quite a fast speed. Then, at the end of the eighteenth century, Charles Babbage was born and, at the age of thirty, was telling the British Royal Astronomical Society that he could build a pilot model of a machine that would calculate logarithms. One year later he showed it to the assembled Society and was awarded the Society's first gold medal. This inspired Babbage to set to work on a full-scale working version of the machine. Despite the help of Lady Lovelace, who was inspired by a Frenchman, Joseph-Marie Jacquard, whose punched card looms can still be found in some British factories, Babbage's programmable computer never worked. His ideas were taken up by a Swedish engineer called George Scheutz who set out to build his own version of Babbage's machine. This did work and was shown at an engineering exhibition in 1855. The unfortunate Babbage was present to see the success of his rival [14].

Computer technology now moved to the United States, where in 1880 the US government was faced with carrying out its eleventh population census. By 1887 the mass of data had still not been processed and so the government decided to hold a competition for a machine that could handle large amounts of data. The competition was won by Herman Hollerith who produced a tabulating machine. The success of this enabled Hollerith to set up his Tabulating Machine Company which went from strength to strength. In 1911 it merged with a number of other data handling companies to form the Computing, Tabulating and Recording

Company. When Hollerith died in 1929 its name had become the International Business Machine Corporation, or IBM.

The Second World War acted as a further stimulus to development and in 1943 a young man called Howard Aiken, an assistant professor of mathematics at Harvard, was financed by IBM to build the Harvard Mark1 machine. Another pioneering group was located at the Moore School of Engineering in Pennsylvania, and in 1946 their ENIAC machine was switched on. This machine was much more advanced than the Mark1 and ushered in the Computer Age. By the 1950s IBM, Bell Telephone and Sperry-Rand were designing computers for the market place, and in England a team of engineers at Manchester University was completing the building of the first Atlas Computer. Interestingly, on the fringes of this team was a reserved young man called Alan Turing, who died in mysterious circumstances in 1954. Although now hailed as a genius he was unappreciated at Manchester where he was a mathematician in a department of engineers [15]. Another British pioneering effort came from the catering and food processing company, J. Lyons, which branched out into computing to produce Leo. In the 1950s it was used by Littlewood's Mail Order Company in Liverpool for stock control.

The most pervasive piece of office technology until recently, the typewriter, came into offices in 1870s. At this time office work was predominantly a male occupation. By 1900 this had changed and in a US clerical workforce of one million, one in four clerks were now women.

In the 1920s machines invaded every part of the office and some hundred new ones made their appearance every year. These included adding and calculating machines, duplicating and dictating machines and machines for handling a variety of accounting activities. By the 1930s women outnumbered men and this growth of machines and feminization of the office has continued until today [16].

Computers had been in active military use during the Second World War but their penetration into offices took longer. In the US, the Bureau of the Census installed the first UNIVAC machine in 1951 and in the same year the Bank of America introduced a specially designed machine called ERMA to handle the daily operations for 50,000 customer accounts. By 1959 around 2000 computers of all sizes were in use for a variety of business, scientific and engineering purposes.

In Britain the same feminization of office work occurred, with women occupying around 75% of all clerical posts. Computers moved into offices there also and the author's first piece of research into the impact of computers on people took place at the beginning of the 1960s. At this time an international study of the consequences of these new machines was organized by the European Productivity Association. A number of countries took part and, in Britain, the author was able to study the first, faltering steps towards using the new technology taken by a northern bank and a cattle food manufacturer [17].

In the 1960s no-one knew what the impact of computer technology on offices would be and the great fear was that it would cause unemployment. There was a belief, fostered by the media, that the speed and efficiency of these new machines would be so great that large numbers of women and some men would lose their jobs. In fact, it was a considerable time before this prophecy came true. The early machines were so unreliable and so difficult to program that many business organizations found that they were employing more, rather than less, labour as programmers and operators were added to their staffs.

Some new and unpleasant female jobs now appeared on the scene. One was punch operating. Large numbers of women were required to punch the cards or paper tape that provided input to the new computers. This job, while extremely boring, required considerable accuracy and so provided a new manifestation of a job hardly fit for humans. While shop-floor assembly jobs had always been dull and demanding, at least the women doing them had been able to talk to each other across the moving line. The new computer work was both monotonous and required concentration. To add insult to injury, as the technology developed women found that the speed at which they worked was being recorded by the their own machines. Too slow a pace meant loss of pay or even dismissal.

Generally then, for women if not for men, these early computer-associated jobs reduced rather than increased job satisfaction. Work that in its manual form had a degree of interest, and might require some problem solving and decision taking, became routinized and also segmented. Instead of being responsible for a sequence of activities, women were limited to preparing input for the computer or correcting errors in its output. The fear of job loss through redundancy also became stronger in offices employing large numbers of female staff. In time computers did increasingly displace clerks, although in both America and Europe growing economies meant that, for a while, new jobs would replace the old.

Two factors led to the routinization and segmentation of clerical jobs. First, the primitive nature of early computer systems encouraged technical designers to focus on the needs of the computer and ignore the needs of people. An information systems specialist, Harold Sackman, explained the ideology of the technical systems analysts of the time.

Early computers were virtually one of a kind, very expensive to build and operate. Computer time was far more expensive than human time. Under these constraints, it was essential that computer efficiency came first, with people last.... Technical matters turned computer professionals on; human matters turned them off. Users were troublesome petitioners somewhere at the end of the line who had to be satisfied with what they got [18].

While the new computer specialists were not concerned about people, the influence of Taylorism flourished in work study and organization and methods departments. Here the philosophy was still one of reducing the influence of the worker by breaking work down into a series of simple and repetitive tasks, each task being undertaken by a different individual. The logic behind this continued to be that it increased production and saved money. Clerks on simple clerical jobs received low pay and were easily replaceable if they left the firm. Computers provided a new vehicle for this philosophy by their ability to handle complex numerical transactions, leaving the human being with the simple, routine tasks.

This focus on the technical at the expense of the human has, in some areas, continued to the present day. Some technologists still try to remove the human being from the systems that they design, even when it has been demonstrated that a person can perform a complex task better than the machine. Some monotonous data input jobs still remain and a number of British companies have been sued by their female employees for repetitive strain injury. But both the culture and the technology are changing. Modern technology requires an intelligent, skilled workforce and the principles of Taylorism are losing their strength. It has always been possible to offer employees either freedom or constraint. Today the business advantages of flexibility and freedom are increasingly being recognized and accepted.

The development of systems design

Systems analysis, the term until recently most commonly applied to the design of systems incorporating computers, emerged as a result of war-time knowledge and experience that was later taken over by industry. During the Second World War its forerunner was known as 'operations analysis' and took the form of a systematic approach to assist decision takers to deal with complex problems. Operations analysis required:

- a careful definition of the objectives that were to be realized;
- an identification and comparison of the alternative means by which these objectives could be achieved and the costs and benefits of each alternative;
- a selection of the strategy most likely to achieve the desired results – given resource constraints, and an assessment of the success of the chosen strategy.

Operations analysis was pioneered by the Rand Corporation which was working on weapon development for the US Air Force. The approach proved so successful that in 1961 Defense Secretary Robert S. McNamara introduced it throughout the Defense Department and into all the armed services. The American government also recognised the value of a systematic approach to complex decision taking. In 1965 President Johnson directed that a similar approach – called PPBS (Planned-Programming-Budgeting Systems) – should be introduced into all Federal Government departments.

US industry's interest in operations analysis was awakened in the 1950s through a growing concern about the difficulty of taking decisions in complex environments. Large companies began using approaches similar to that developed by Rand which they called 'systems analysis'. They saw these as ways of substituting a rational weighing of alternatives and consequences for the hunches and rule-of-thumb methods that they had previously used. The Ford Motor Company was one of these firms. Its President, Arjay Miller, described systems analysis as an excellent means for handling the problems of business and as a way of distributing responsibility for decision taking to larger groups of people [19].

Systems analysis, defined very broadly as a means for solving complex business problems, attracted increasing attention and generated much interest and enthusiasm. This interest was not confined to government and industry. Daniel Bell, who in 1967, was chairman of a commission forecasting what would happen by the year 2000, saw the approach as a means for addressing some of the larger problems of society. It would enable society to choose its own path in the light of its own values.

Systems analysis then started off in its early form as a novel, comprehensive way of handling complex problems operating in conditions of uncertainty. It was seen by the early practitioners as providing a sense of direction and a means for intelligent, effective choice that would take account of important social values. It was to be flexible, democratic and evolving, in contrast to the use of coercive or authoritarian power as a means for getting things done.

But new ideas change, are rethought and become operationalized in different forms and this was true of systems analysis. Rand, and the engineers and mathematicians that were influenced by its thinking, sought to make systems analysis more precise and mathematical. They called their work 'operational research' and other new names such heuristics, decision theory and systems design appeared in the literature. An important group, influenced by ideas from Europe as well as the US, set about trying to achieve a general theory of systems – a language with which systems could be described. These developments took place in the 1950s, and an influential centre was the Rand Corporation in Los Angeles. The group there sought to identify a set of properties and functions common to all systems which could be mathematically modelled. These seekers after a general systems theory did not usually include the awkward variable – people and their behaviour – in their models. This may be the reason why an acceptable general systems theory has still not been found.

Another group, also influenced by the thinking of European scientists, defined systems which included people as 'open' and 'living'. They used these terms to describe systems which interacted with their environment, and they believed that successful systems analysis required an understanding and characterization of the systems environment. An influential group that looked at systems in this way was based at the Tavistock Institute in London after the Second World War. Their work led to the development of socio-technical theory – an approach which takes account of both human needs and technical requirements when systems are being designed, and tries to optimize both.

While the debate between the 'general systems' and 'open systems' theorists was taking place, computers were moving into industry at an increasingly rapid rate and methods were required to assist their successful introduction. It was clear that a computer could not just be dropped into the middle of a firm or department and the 'on' button pressed. Nothing at all would happen. Careful thought must be given to what the computer could and should be used for and to the reorganization of the business activities which its introduction would affect. A simple, practical form of systems analysis was therefore an urgent necessity for this new technology.

The term 'systems analysis' has always seemed narrow for the range of activities associated with it. Analysis implies the breaking down of things into small parts, whereas introducing technical systems requires the creation of new structures once the original problem has been understood and defined. Systems design seems a more appropriate description for today's activities. This, in turn, must be associated with organizational design. The new phrase 'business process re-engineering' (BPR) attempts encompass both of these activities, but leaves an impression that the focus of interest is machines rather than people.

There are many definitions of design. It has been described as 'devising artefacts to attain goals' and as 'simulating what we want to do (or make) before we do (or make) it' [20]. But statements of this kind are not very helpful. They tell us something of what design is aiming to achieve, but little about the important and necessary processes that have to be set up and managed before the result is achieved. These processes are complex when computer-based systems are being designed to solve business problems. They involve the use of tools, techniques, ideas, information and knowledge. Design also requires creativity, for in the computer world there is usually no 'one best way' of achieving the goals that have been set for a system. It is greatly influenced by the philosophies and values of the individuals and groups involved in the design task and these have at their disposal a confusing array of methods, methodologies and concepts. All can help the designer gain some control over a mass of variables, but because the use of one rather than another may influence the nature of the goals that are achieved, they need to be selected with care.

Design methods

A method is a way of doing things and can incorporate a number of tools to assist the analysis of the business problem or the development of a solution. The word methodology really means the study of methods but, in practice, designers often use it to describe a collection of methods. An example of a method in favour today is prototyping – in which a model of the system is built and tested before the final system is implemented.

Most designers work with a set of principles derived from experience and good practice which guide their approach. They may strive for 'simplicity' – the simplest design that meets the problem specification; or for 'flexibility' – a system that can easily be altered to meet new problems and needs [21]. Systems designers can also have a multiplicity of objectives that they are striving to achieve. As well as creating a system that successfully addresses a business problem, they may also aim to produce one that has certain characteristics – for example, one that is reliable, maintainable, efficient, secure and user-centred.

Methods and methodologies have always been seen as a useful way of bringing order and logic into the design process and as devices to assist training. But because systems design has been defined as a technical activity, traditional methods have been tools and procedures for designing technical systems. The systems analyst has not seen his role as helping with the management of complex change. He has restricted this to providing technical solutions.

Because of this narrow view the practice of systems design has generally been broken down into a number of sequential operations. Typically, these have included analysis – gaining an understanding of the problem that has to be addressed and describing the activities, data and information flow associated with it. This led to a requirements definition. Next came a specification or description of the functions to be performed by the system to process the required data. Design followed, and this covered the development of the internal structure of the software which would provide the functions that had been specified. Implementation was the development of the computer code that would enable the system to produce data. Validation checked that each stage was successfully accomplished and 'evolution' was the correction of errors or modification of the system to meet new needs [22].

Until recently, the human user of the system figured very little in this technical approach. Consideration was not given to issues which are regarded as of prime importance today – business goals, needs and structures, competing demands for information, multiple interest groups and dynamic and complex business environments.

Now, things are changing and it is increasingly being recognized that a purely technical approach to systems design is not sufficient. A great deal of attention is being paid to the development of methods that will enable systems designers and users to take account of business and organizational issues. These are sometimes called 'soft system' methodologies because they are as concerned with people as with technology. The author of this book has developed one called ETHICS which is described in Appendix A of this book [23]. This regards organizational improvement and employee job satisfaction as being as important as technical development. Another method with similar objectives has been developed by Checkland [24].

Because human, organizational and technical factors are increasingly recognized as having to be taken account of, today's design ideally requires the coordinated effort of a multidisciplinary team. This team will have to be carefully and sympathetically managed if its creativity is to be stimulated and maintained. Tight controls and bureaucracy will almost certainly be counter-productive and an environment which provides challenge, work freedom and opportunities for initiative is the one most likely to produce high quality design.

Designing systems for institutions and their employees is a heavy responsibility. Because technology can have such a dramatic effect on the human condition we need to think very carefully about how we use it and what we use it for. Schumacher in his famous book *Small is Beautiful* wrote

> Technology tends to develop its own laws and principles, and these are very different from those of human nature or living nature .... The primary task of technology is to lighten the burden of work man has to carry in order to stay alive and develop his potential [25].

There is increasing concern that technology shall be introduced and used in a humanistic way, with beneficiaries rather than victims. Systems designers have a major part to play in ensuring that technology is designed to have a positive and liberating effect.

Future developments

Some interesting questions are: What happens as technology moves on and the face-to-face group is replaced by the remote group in which each individual is at a different location and conversation is through electronic messaging systems? Can user-led design still be striven for, even though it takes a different form? How can participation, communication, choice and freedom continue to evolve as electronic conferencing increasingly becomes the norm?

There are some positive developments here. New applications to support teamwork and participation are appearing on the business scene. Electronic mail, bulletin boards, and conferencing systems already provide a basic infrastructure for communication and collaborative working. It is also being suggested that the anonymity of electronic messaging can improve the quality of communication. This will be less influenced by power relations than it is in the face-to-face context and this can reduce the obstacles to free and unrestrained inquiry. Others maintain that we are moving towards a network nation in which vast amounts of information and socio-emotional communications will be exchanged with colleagues, friends and strangers who live in distant places and whom we rarely meet [26].

But other writers see problems ahead. They point out that computer conversations bear little relationship to face-to-face conversations. In the first place they are written, not spoken. They extend the writing domain to cover areas of communication that until now were restricted to face-to-face interaction, mail and telephone. This is a major change. The communicators now become sexless and faceless, their personalities are diminished to what they write and they have no hierarchical positions. In other words they are not 'real' people. There is also the possibility of 'silent rejection'. Today, those who use electronic mail are frequently anxious that their messages will elicit no response and many individuals are casual about replying to electronic messages even though they would not react the same way to verbal messages.

It is argued that this impersonality may free people from taboos. For example, systems now exist which act as dating agencies, although the partners never meet. There are others in which one can talk about anything to whoever one wants, all subjects being acceptable. This may be truly 'freedom of speech' but it can also be a game of masks and disguises in which the real is person is never known [27].

Technology has always offered a promise of Utopia and a threat of disaster, John Bunyan's Promised Land and his Slough of Despond. What actually happens depends on our values, priorities and needs as well as who is taking the decisions. Tomorrow's information systems can improve our work, our social interaction and our personal and group freedom, provided that we make informed and socially responsible choices. Social responsibility requires a knowledge of what people want and what they regard as improvement. This, in turn, requires mutual understanding and shared meanings and these are achieved through good communication in which all can take part. Lastly, progress requires a common set of values, norms and beliefs, in which freedom to choose and freedom from unwanted constraints and hardships are priorities to be striven for.

References

1.   Mumford, L., *The Pentagon of Power*, Secker and Warburg, 1964.
2.   Smith, A., *The Wealth of Nations*, Penguin, 1979.
3.   Markus,T., *Buildings and Power*, Routledge, 1993.
4.   Fox, A., *Beyond Contract: Work, Power and Trust Relations*, Faber, 1974.
5.   Bentham, J., *An Introduction to the Principles of Morals and Legislation*, in *Works* (ed. J. Bowring), William Tait, 1838-43.
6.   Mumford, L., op. cit.
7.   Babbage, C., *On the Economuy of Machinery and Manufacturers*, Knight, 1835.
8.   Fox, A., op. cit.
9.   Mumford, L. op. cit.
10. Taylor, F.W., *Scientific Management*, Harper and Row, 1947.
11. Davis, L. and Taylor, J.C., *The Design of Jobs*, Penguin, 1972.
12. Bell, D., *The Coming of Post-industrial Society*, Heinemann, 1974.
13. Drucker, P., 'The age of social transformation', in *The Atlantic Monthly*, pp. 53-80, November 1994.
14. Evans, C., *The Mighty Micro*, Victor Gollancz, 1979.
15. Ibid.
16. Baker, E.F., *Technology and Woman's Work*, Columbia University Press, 1964.

17. Mumford, E and Banks, O., *The Computer and the Clerk*, Routledge and Kegan Paul, 1967.
18. Sackman, H., *Mass Information Utilities and Social Excellence*, Auerbach, 1971.
19. Mumford, E. and Macdonald, B., *XSEL's Progress*, Wiley, 1989.
20. Ibid.
21. Leech, D.J. and Turner, B.T., *Engineering Design for Profit*, Ellis Horwood, 1985.
22. Wasserman, A., Freeman, P., and Porcella, M. 'Characteristics of software development methodologies' in T.W.Olle, H.G.Sol, and C.J.Tully (eds) *Information Systems Design Methodologies: a Feature Analysis*, North Holland, 1983.
23. Mumford, E., *Effective Systems Design and Requirements Analysis*, Macmillan Press, 1995.
24. Checkland, P., *Systems Thinking, Systems Practice*, Wiley, 1981.
25. Schumacher, E.F., *Small is Beautiful*, Abacus Little, Brown, 1987.
26. Poster, M., *The Mode of Information*, Polity Press, 1990.
27. Ibid.

2 Systems designers and the ethics of design

This chapter addresses the question of how systems designers can be assisted to adopt an ethical position when designing and implementing new systems. It discusses how the philosophers of the past and the biologists of today define the notion of human improvement and some of the dilemmas of an ethical approach. It considers the role of the moral leader and strategies that can assist an ethical approach. It concludes by providing two sets of questions that can help the systems designer to provide an approach that is ethically beneficial for both users and employers.

Philosophy and ethics

Today there is much talk about market forces, efficiency and profits, but there is little discussion of ethics – what we need to do to preserve and improve this world, its institutions and all the people who live on the planet. This is in contrast to earlier times when a great deal of thought was given to these subjects, especially as they applied to man and his behaviour.

Yet, although few of us have clearly thought out philosophies of desired behaviour, we all have some kind of vision of the world which helps to explain the events we experience, and guides our thinking on which of the activities around us we should welcome and approve of and which we should deplore and reject. Many of these responses will be derived from religion, from our view of the state and its responsibilities and from notions of freedom and democracy. Others, particularly if we are scientists or engineers will be derived from biology, physics, mathematics and associated scientific subjects.

The greater part of the models that we use to explain what goes on around us are those that provide reassuring and comfortable explanations that fit our prejudices and desire for security. But, if we are unhappy, confused, frustrated or full of aggression, our models of the world will contain many negative visions of things that we would like to change.

We can always learn a great deal from the past and so it is useful to begin by examining the ideas of some of the early philosophers on the conditions required for human development and ethical progress. Most believed that progress equalled improvement. They thought that man had the capacity to develop himself and his environment so that things became 'better'. By better they meant becoming more knowledgeable and more in control, so that human beings could have happier and more satisfactory lives.

One of the earliest and most influential of thinkers was Plato who lived around 300 B.C. [1]. He believed that there was a natural leaning towards justice; that most people wanted order and discipline, both in their minds and in the community in which they lived. Because of this need, children must be educated into becoming rational and just creatures, and a social environment must be created appropriate for that purpose.

In the seventeenth and eighteenth centuries there was a proliferation of great philosophical and political theorists who suggested ways in which man could be assisted to develop to a higher state. Jean-Jacques Rousseau, for example, had a great deal in common with Plato [2]. He too saw man as a rational and moral being who wanted to live well by his own standards. He believed that people cared deeply about freedom because they were essentially moral and had notions of excellence. Freedom provided men with greater opportunities to become better citizens and to live worthwhile lives.

Whereas Bentham later associated happiness with wealth Rousseau saw man as having a concept of happiness that related to freedom. To be happy meant being on good terms with oneself and with others. To be on good terms with oneself required good relationships with others and these, in turn, depended on the right kind of social situations. For Rousseau, happiness as distinct from pleasure was only possible if men were self-conscious and moral beings. Rousseau believed that the right kind of society was a society of equals in which people obeyed laws which were seen as just and moral. Discipline made people perfect. Through it they became at peace with themselves and with others.

Many other philosophers of the same period had similar ideas. David Hume believed in enlightened self-love [3]. He preached 'You will respect others because you respect yourself. You will want to rely on others so that they can rely on you.' This is a similar concept to the new communitarianism offered as a solution to today's problems by the American behavioural scientist, Amitai Etzioni [4]. Hume, like many philosophers of his time, believed that the rule of law was required to assist justice and legitimize these social values.

Montesquieu and Locke were two more liberal political thinkers of the period [5]. Both saw the state and its legislation playing an important part in the creation of conditions for freedom. John Locke took this a stage further, arguing that men are only moral because they have been disciplined by society. They are made moral in the process of adapting themselves to society. In his view the natural obligation of an adult man to other men is not to injure them. He should treat his associates as he would want to be treated himself.

In the nineteenth century John Stuart Mill was one of the most influential philosophers and thinkers [6]. He believed strongly in rational thinking and thought that the ability to do this was an expression of freedom. He also believed that a free individual was likely to contribute to the positive development of society. His aim was to create the establishment of a healthy society. This required a body of definitive opinions on what was right, reached by agreed, rational reasoning.

Mill saw education and culture as important aids to higher development. In his opinion the more intelligent should set the tone of the society in which they lived. The objective of this development was to maximize both the happiness of the individual and the happiness of society as a whole. This happiness would come primarily from moral altruism and intellectual progress. Its attainment required individual freedom so that men could seek out moral truth. Mill was dedicated to the establishment of a society in which all opinions were tolerated, education was important and men had responsibility for their actions.

In the twentieth century, positive political thinkers of this power and influence have not been plentiful or obvious. We have experienced Lenin, Mao, Hitler and others, but their influence and moral codes have not proved benign. It can be argued that this gap has left many of us with a moral vacuum which politicians, the Church and educational establishments have been unable to fill. There is now an urgent need for a discussion of societal values, moral decisions and ethical strategies which can help us to address today's problems. At present we have a diversity of movements, all pressing their particular single-issue interests. These include the Green movement, the Gay movement, Animal Rights and many others. We also have a diversity of problems ranging from world-wide unemployment to the contents of McDonald's hamburgers.

Can scientists and technologists lead or influence this ethical discourse? Some have already done so. The French philosopher/scientist and priest Teilhard de Chardin, who died in New York in 1955, tried to cross the boundary between ethics and science by studying the development of man as a member of society and his development as a biological being [7]. For Teilhard de Chardin evolution was a straight line progressing towards a pre-set and determined goal which could be called human improvement. He saw the hope of the world as lying in its future and this future depending on men doing their utmost to speed up their own evolution – evolution meaning the development of intelligence as well as bodily adaptation. He was searching for a set of values which had reality and were relevant to the world in which we live. He saw this as a world of nature, of biology, of personality and also as a world of hope, of longing and of achievement.

Biology and ethics

Today's biologists are playing an increasingly influential role in the development of ideas about society. Unlike the early philosophers they focus not on what should be happening but on what is happening. They are not trying to make sense of the world through philosophical argument, they are trying to gain under-standing through observation and scientific experiment.

But in the biological model change is not given a moral dimension. It is seen as a reaction to the environment which, if well judged, will reinforce stability and avoid upheaval. The belief here is that dysfunctional conflict with high costs and few benefits should always be reduced in the interests of the survival of the species.

When attempts are being made to understand and explain complex phenomena such as the contribution of ethical behaviour to human development and progress, biology may help us to throw light on dark corners. Biology, like philosophy, is concerned with understanding development, although it is the development of living organisms, not political, organizational and social structures and ideas.

Biologists argue that most species have what are called 'evolutionary stable strategies' [8]. This is defined as a strategy which, if most members of a population adopt it, cannot be bettered by an alternative strategy. However, there may also be transitional periods of instability which terminate in a new evolutionary stable strategy. Progressive evolution is then not so much a steady upward climb as a series of discrete steps from one stable plateau to another.

It seems possible that culture and human behaviour follow similar progressions. The transmission of culture from one generation to the next, although basically conservative, can also evolve in unexpected ways. The 'hippie' culture of the 1960s may be an example, as may be the variety of pressure and religious groups of today. This variety may enable us to deal more effectively with today's complexity.

The biologist Richard Dawkins suggests that culture evolves in the same way as genes. Ideas, fashions, methods, which Dawkins calls 'memes', propagate themselves by moving from brain to brain by a process of 'imitation' or 'copying' [9]. If a scientist hears or reads about a good idea, he or she passes it on to his colleagues and students and refers to it in articles and lectures. The brain then becomes the vehicle for 'memes' propagation. Memes survive if they have psychological appeal. However, some are more successful than others at doing this. Why this is the case is an interesting question for research.

Biologists believe that the multiplication and spread of genes is more important than the length of time that they survive. This may also be true of 'memes'. Dawkins suggests that if the meme is a scientific idea its spread will depend upon how acceptable it is to the population of individual scientists. Some memes, like genes, achieve brilliant short-term success but they soon fade away. Management fashions such as 'total quality' and 'business process re-engineering' may be examples of this tendency.

Selection favours memes that exploit their cultural environment to their own advantage, the memes' cultural environment being other memes. For example, when industry is focused on improving efficiency, all memes which are seen as contributing to this will be actively transmitted from one brain to another. However, Dawkins recognizes that there is a logical difficulty in this explanation of how ideas are transmitted. This is that man has a capacity for foresight and for altruism. Man can see and understand long-term interests, which genes and memes cannot. He can rebel against the selfish gene or meme. Evolutionary psychologists explain this by introducing the factor of 'social organization'. For many species, and both men and ants come into this category, gene and meme survival depend on organizational fitness as well as individual fitness. Through social organization we develop social bonds to facilitate the social co-operation necessary for the organizations successful survival. Altruism expresses and reinforces these bonds and therefore contributes to the organization's success. This results in ethical behaviour [10].

Biologists argue that an antagonistic world occurs where a change in the fitness of one species is balanced by an equal but opposite change in the fitness of all interacting species. This principle can also be applied to social organization. If a group dedicated to 'order' has to interact with other groups dedicated to disorder, then the first group is likely to be traumatized and may have difficulty in surviving. Communitarianism is only possible when interacting groups are not too far apart in their objectives and behaviour. The hippie communities of the 1960s, who were early practitioners of communitarianism and represented what Marcuse called 'the great refusal', were an example of this principle [11].

How relevant are these ideas to systems design?

It can be argued that both political philosophy and biology can provide the ethical systems designer with greater understanding of the formation and communication of ethical principles. Political philosophy provides a history of ideas about morality and shows how these have changed over the years, moving first from a focus on the state as arbiter and controller of ethics to a concentration on the individual. And moving again in today's world from the individual to a recognition of the importance of the social group.

Biology provides an explanation of why we behave as we do. If we are able to accept that there are parallels between the development of a species and the development of society then we can learn a number of lessons. One is that the present turbulent environment is unlikely to endure. We will eventually return to stability, although this stability may be of a different kind from that which we have known in the past. A second lesson is that powerful ideas, powerful in the sense that they are psychologically acceptable at a particular period of time, will spread rapidly, although they may not last very long. Also, that as they spread they will become distorted and the original message may be lost. A third lesson is that if a group is developing in a particular way, but the groups with which it interacts are developing in a very different ways, then it will be in an antagonistic environment and may not survive. There is a lesson here for politicians as well as for systems designers. It can be argued that prosperity both provides and requires stability and a reduction of risk. Stable governments provide law and order and ensure that contracts are legally enforceable. Unstable governments are unable to do this. Stable governments are also more likely to be prosperous. As a rule, the more stable and peaceful a society, the greater its financial assets relative to its tangible assets. Yet, if the biological analogy is correct, even a stable society will not be able to avoid periods of turbulence.

Instability occurs when a government loses the confidence of its people and is likely to fall.

What is ethical responsibility?

Since very early times, in most societies it has been believed that if people are to be good citizens then they require ethical and moral codes to guide their behaviour, although these may differ from one group to another and from one time period to another [12]. Ethics is about making choices – often in situations where there are constraints on what is or is not permissible, or where the outcomes are not clear. Ethical problems do not appear to change very much with time, although the nature of the choices and available solutions may take very different forms.

Scientists and technologists have particular ethical responsibilities because their work can have a major impact on the world we live in. Yet they are frequently required to use their own judgement on what is ethical behaviour. For many issues there are no institutional codes or rules of conduct. This is particularly true when these issues relate to new technology where consequences may be unclear or even unknown. Occasionally, they have to act swiftly and become whistle blowers when new ethical dilemmas suddenly arise. Generally, it is war that has brought scientists some of their most difficult ethical dilemmas, particularly with reference to weapons of mass destruction, such as biological and chemical warfare and the atomic bomb.

In the scientific community, the medical specialist has better defined ethical codes than most other groups. Most doctors have a clear objective related to saving life or restoring health and the penalties for unacceptable behaviour are documented in the Hippocratic Oath. They are also enforced by powerful sanctions, such as expulsion from the medical profession if serious infringements occur. These codes support ethical principles and protect the group from external attack. But they may also restrict entry to groups and individuals who are seen as willing and able to join.

Many other professions, including the British Computer Society, have also drawn up ethical codes, but these are often vague and difficult to apply and enforce. For example, must an engineer give precedence to the needs of clients or to the needs of society as a whole? Must a manager pay attention to the needs of employees or is he or she solely concerned with profits for shareholders?

The Greeks believed that knowledge and values were inseparable. Knowledge brought with it the ability to act correctly as a citizen. Today, we view the situation as more complicated, recognizing that while knowledge can often be said to be neutral, the application of knowledge can often, at one and the same time, have both beneficial and potentially dangerous consequences. Atomic energy is a current example. Ethical responsibilities will also vary, both with the nature of the work that is being carried out and the nature of the social environment where the work is conducted.

The critic who wishes to protest at what he or she regards as unethical behaviour or events has a number of options. One is to 'exit' from the situation, either by refusing to purchase or use the unethical product, or by leaving a job which is seen as ethically compromising [13]. This option was used by British scientists in the Second World War, a number of whom refused to work in industries associated with weapon production. But it is a difficult option to apply today when jobs are scarce.

A second option is the vocal one of complaining. In the past, trade unions have often protected questioning workers; today their weakness means that they are less able to do so. However, powerful groups working in a united way can still make their voices heard and professional associations can assist this. Doctors, hospital and community nurses and midwives have all used this weapon recently, and the British national health service has accepted the legitimacy of 'whistle-blowing', provided certain procedures are followed. Medical staff are also debating whether to stick with complaining or take the 'exit' option by going on strike. They define their problem as both a practical and an ethical one. They want higher pay, but they are also protesting at what they see as a deterioration in the human values of the health service. The dilemma here is that their strategies for achieving the first may exacerbate the problems of the second.

The moral leader

People who are uncertain how to behave in new situations where values and consequences are unclear often welcome some ethical guidance and here the role of a moral leader can be helpful. The characteristics of such a person have been discussed by Jürgen Habermas, John Rawls and many other philosophers [14]. Rawls suggests that there can be a 'moral point of view'. This involves being impartial, or not taking sides; getting general agreement on moral issues, while accepting that situations change and what is seen as moral at one time may be viewed as immoral at another. Once there is agreement, people should be told that 'This is what you must do.' Rawls calls these impartiality, universalization, reversibility and prescriptivity [15]. Ideally, this moral point of view is created as a result of discussion amongst groups of individuals who are equal partners in the solution of an ethical problem.

Gordon Burnand offers some strategies likely to encourage an ethical approach [16]. The first of these is *clarification* – making clear the moral principles which the group is trying to apply. Many companies do this through value statements related to the personnel policies they wish to administer and the behaviour they require from their staff. Here follows an example of the value statement of 4C International, a new software firm based in Rotterdam in the Netherlands. It employed thirty staff, twelve of whom were highly skilled systems developers. At an early stage in its history it decided to involve all staff in creating a statement of company values. Each member of staff first listed the values he or she believed to be important. A meeting of all staff then agreed the content and presentation of the final published statement which is set out below.

4C VALUES
A Statement of Guiding Principles for Relations
with Colleagues and Clients

These guiding principles have been derived from the suggestions made by 4C staff on how they would like to relate to each other in the work situation and to the external clients they service.

RELATIONS WITH COLLEAGUES

ESTABLISHING AND MAINTAINING GOOD RELATIONS

SHARED VALUES
4C aims to create a set of values which all staff share, follow and develop. These values include an acceptance of the Company's mission and objectives and an appreciation of the dedication of others.

COMMITMENT
4C will try to create a high quality organization with challenging jobs which provide job satisfaction. This will assist staff to be fully professional in all that they do.

TRUST
Our aim will be to develop mutual trust, confidence and friendship between colleagues, managers and clients.

CO-OPERATION
A high priority will be placed on co-operation. Strategies and procedures will be introduced to help it to flourish. Co-operation should assist the achievement of personal, group and company goals.

COMMUNICATION
Staff will be provided with as much information as possible about 4C's present and future business opportunities, intentions and plans. Staff will be encouraged to communicate their views on all relevant subjects to management and their other colleagues.

CREATIVITY
All members of the organization will be encouraged to provide and be receptive to new ideas and to constructive criticism. These will be actively sought and implemented.

All very 'KM'!

FUN
Whenever possible the work should be fun.

STAFF DEVELOPMENT

RECRUITMENT
4C will strive to hire, develop and retain the best people available irrespective of race, gender, age, etc.

PERSONAL DEVELOPMENT
Every effort will be made to provide opportunities for personal development and the achievement of professional goals.

INITIATIVE
Personal and professional initiative will be encouraged as much as possible.

WORK ENVIRONMENT

WORK ORGANIZATION
Every attempt will be made to provide a flexible, well organized, environment that fosters quality and innovation.

RELATIONSHIPS WITH CLIENTS

ESTABLISHING AND MAINTAINING GOOD RELATIONS WITH CLIENTS

CLIENT NEEDS
Client needs will be the principal driving force behind 4C's activities. Every effort will be made to develop and maintain 4C's strong Client orientation.

ENSURING 4C'S PROFITABILITY

STRATEGY
There will be a continual search for new ways to improve productivity. Efforts will be made to increase product and process innovation, product diversification, the extension of market areas and other means to improve our 'competitive edge'.

STRUCTURE
4C will aim to have an organization structure that promotes and sustains growth, flexibility and high performance.

Value statements of this kind bring with them certain requirements. First, senior management must accept and apply them. Second, there must be some rewards for those who implement them with sincerity, and some penalties for those who do not. These can be material. For example, merit awards or promotion, or they can be psychological, based on shown approval or disapproval.

Once values have been agreed and established Burnand points out that they must be maintained and reinforced. He accepts Rawls's view that this requires a degree of *impartiality* regarding what is right and wrong in particular situations. External mediators may sometimes be a help here, as they are not caught up in the internal politics of the situations.

coaches?

Consistency is another necessary strategy. The values and rules must be maintained over time. They should be written down, and known and accepted by a majority of staff. Procedures and archives can sometimes help to ensure that *fair comparisons* are made between one problem situation and another. But, if there are no available comparisons, then ethical issues have to be settled 'on their merits'. Decisions will now be a product of the personal ethical positions of the participants. In all situations it is important to take account of *intentions* and *consequences* – what people are trying to achieve and the result of their actions. Accidental deviations can then be ignored or treated as of little importance.

Empathy is also a necessary characteristic for any person or group confronted with ethical problems. The ability to put oneself in another person's shoes, and to understand rather than judge. *Tradition* is also important. If a system has been successfully operating for some time then it is likely to be seen by most people as reasonable and fair.

All groups, technical professionals, management and trades unions, although their objectives may differ, should always strive to be moral leaders in the work situation. They should set an example, persuade others of the importance of moral principles and build up credibility and trust by always being consistent. They should also see it as an important part of their role to train others to be concerned about ethical problems.

Ethics in hard times

All of this may not be too difficult in situations of employment stability. It is much more difficult in times of high unemployment, when redundancy is an always present threat. Today, we have the novel and threatening situation of unemployment rising in economic recovery as well as in recession. We have a situation of what has been called 'jobless growth' [17].

Figures produced by the International Labour Office, and reported in *The European*, on 6 July 1995, tell us that in 1994 thirty per cent of the global labour force, about 800 million people were unemployed, with around 35 million workers out of work in industrialized countries. The ILO Director General, Michel Hansenne, described this as both morally unacceptable and economically irrational. Figures produced by Frank Field, Chairman of the British House of Commons Social Services Select Committee, show that the structure of employment has changed in the UK [18]. Out of a total work force of 24.6 million, 6.5 million are part-time workers and, of this 6.5 million, 5.2 million are women.

If large numbers are losing their jobs then social contracts may lose their value and be replaced by suspicion and hostility. Social cohesion and an adherence to ethical principles require feelings of basic justice to be shared by all members of a group. These have been described as 'rights, liberties and opportunities' [19]. This could mean that in the future we may have to focus more on values outside work, on the importance of community and family.

But for those fortunate enough to have jobs, ethics and their application will still be important. They may be even more important than in the past, because more is at stake. They will need to cover subjects such as how much stress is permissible in the work situation, who is chosen for redundancy and how these individuals are assisted to move easily into an acceptable new life situation, either in another job or in their own community.

Ethical principles are particularly difficult to develop and apply when times are hard, as economic pressures tend to override others. Ethics in hard times is likely to require self-sacrifice and altruism [20]. The Thatcher morality focused very much on the importance of the individual; today, we need a new morality focused on the needs of groups and society. Etzioni's 'communitarianism' is one attempt at encouraging this through its stress on the notion of reciprocity and responsibility for others. We shall look at these problems again in the next chapter.

A further challenge today is the dominance of technical rationality in organizational and government thinking. Government and industrial decisions are increasingly concerned with technical subjects [21]. Yet, despite our increasing knowledge of human and organizational consequences, many scientists still tend to think that most problems can be solved by technical solutions, and that problems should be treated solely on their technical merits.

Ethics and the individual

What guidance can we give to the individual systems designer or computer technologist who wishes to behave in an ethical way when dealing with users and customers? The first thing is that values, although influenced by the groups and cultures that an individual is associated with, are very much a personal thing. Each of us is likely to have our own definition of what is right and wrong and what we should strive to achieve in our relationship with others. The second thing is that we are not usually entirely free agents. If we have employers and colleagues then our attitudes and actions will be affected by the views and demands of these other parties. All of these factors require us to make choices when in situations where we have some freedom of action.

Those systems designers who take a broadly humanistic approach to their relationships with others may find an ethical check-list of value and this is what this section provides. This check-list is derived from the work of an American sociologist, Talcott Parsons, who created a theory of action to guide individuals trying to decide how to behave in particular situations [22].

Parsons suggests that the choices that an individual makes can be split into five categories. These cover the following:

Companies too!

- Whether to go for an immediate gratification of a need or to defer this in the expectation of some long-term gain. (affectivity v. affective neutrality)
- Whether to place more importance on personal interests or on wider group interests. (self-orientation v. collectivity orientation)
- Whether to respond to a situation in conformity with accepted practice or treat each situation on its merits. (universalism v. particularism)
- Whether to respond to individuals because of who they are or because of what they do. (ascription v. achievement)
- Whether to respond to similar situations in the same way or to try and identify the differences between each situation. (specificity v. diffuseness).

These pattern variables have been reinterpreted by the author as a series of implicit contracts between the employer and the employee. These are:

	The employee	The organization
The *Knowledge* contract	Wishes the skills and knowledge he or she brings with them to be used and developed	Needs a certain level of skill and knowledge in its employees if it is to function efficiently
The *Psychological* contract	Seeks to further personal interests	Needs employees who are motivated to look after its interests
The *Efficiency* contract	Seeks a work situation in which controls and support services assist personal efficiency	Needs to implement generalized quality and output standards
The *Task Structure* contract	Seeks a set of tasks that meet personal needs for interest, variety and challenge	Needs employees who will accept technical and organizational constraints and requirements

The *Value* contract	Seeks to work for an employer whose values do not contravene his or her own	Needs employees who will accept its ethics and values

From the employee's point of view the knowledge and psychological contracts are associated with needs related to his or her *personality*. In contrast the efficiency and task contracts describe the characteristics of the individual's *role*. The *value* contract is the factor that integrates these personality and role requirements. The values of the employing organization will influence the extent to which it is sympathetic to both the personality and work structure requirements of the individual [23].

These contracts can now be reformulated as a set of questions to be asked and answered by a systems designer who wishes to design a humanistic system that provides the user with a high quality of working life. It has to be recognized that users differ in their needs; however, research has shown that many employees place a high value on the factors listed here.

Questions relating to the user

Knowledge contract
Does the system help the user to apply and develop his or her skills and knowledge? Does it provide an opportunity for significant learning?

Psychological contract
Does the system provide opportunities for positive social interaction? Does it give the user the opportunity to take decisions and assume responsibility? Does it remove or reduce stress? Does it provide job satisfaction?

Efficiency contract
Does the system provide the user with the kind of helpful support that enables him or her to reach high standards of quality and output? For example, through providing relevant, timely and accurate information that is easy to access?

Task structure contract
Has the user been trained to use the system effectively? Does the system provide the user with an acceptable mix of terminal-based and other forms of work? Is the user in control of the system? Is the system easy to use and user friendly?

Value contract
Has the user been consulted about the design and implementation of the system

and been given a sense of ownership? Does the user have fast effective channels for making problems and needs known to technical staff?

As the systems designer is also responsible for providing a system that is efficient and effective from the employer's point of view, a second set of questions can assist this. These are:

Knowledge contract
Today's companies require knowledgeable and flexible employees. Does the system assist the development of these characteristics?

Psychological contract
Does the system, and the way it has been designed and implemented, motivate employees and stimulate them to give high priority to company objectives and interests?

Efficiency contract
Does the system assist the user to meet the efficiency targets and standards required by the company?

Task structure contract
Does the ergonomic design of the system produce a high quality work situation that assists the avoidance of health, absenteeism and labour turnover problems?

Value contract
Do the communication and consultation strategies and procedures associated with the design, implementation and use of the system create a group of high morale users dedicated to furthering the interests of the company?

The systems designer who wishes to combine good technical design with good organizational design and create a system that is both humanistic and advantageous for the employer will try to get as many 'yes' answers as possible to both sides of this equation. The result should be an increasing number of systems that are greeted with enthusiasm and approval by users and which also help the company to develop the skilled, knowledgeable, effective employee labour force that is so important in today's business world.

Two final points need to be made. The first is that technology is never an end in itself. In industry it is a means to making companies more successful in an increasingly competitive environment.

The second is that a well thought out, ethical approach, introduced with goodwill and sincerity, can lead to positive attitudes towards computer technology, a high morale work force at all levels, and a company which has the creativity, motivation and knowledge to compete effectively in tomorrow's world.

References

1. Plamenatz, J., *Man and Society*, Longman, 1963.
2. Ibid.
3. Broad, C.D., *Five Types of Ethical Theory*, Routledge and Kegan Paul, 1979.
4. Etzioni, A., *The Active Society*, Free Press, 1968.
5. Plamenatz, op. cit.
6. Foot, P., *Theories of Ethics*, Oxford University Press, 1967.
7. Jones, D.G., *Teilhard de Chardin: an Analysis and Assessment*, Tyndale Press, 1969.
8. Maynard Smith, J., *Organizational Constraints On The Dynamics Of Evolution*, Manchester University Press, 1990.
9. Dawkins, R., *The Selfish Gene*, Oxford University Press, 1989.
10. Randall, P., Letter to *The Independent* newspaper, 3.5.95.
11. Marcuse, H., *One Dimensional Man*, Beacon, 1964.
12. Lakoff, S.A., *Science and Ethical Responsibility*, Addison-Wesley, 1980.
13. Hirschman, A., *Exit Voice and Loyalty*, Harvard University Press, 1970.
14. Habermas, J., *Moral Consciousness and Communicative Action*, Polity, 1990.
15. Rawls, J., *A Theory of Justice*, Cambridge, Mass., 1971.
16. Burnand, G., *Via Focal Problems*, Leadership Ltd, 1982.
17. Lepenies, W., 'A job to be workwise', *Times Higher Educational Supplement*, 24.3.95.
18. Field, F., *Making Welfare Work*, Institute of Community Studies, 1995.
19. Rawls, op. cit.
20. Callahan, D., 'Minimalist ethics: on the pacification of morality', in A.L. Caplan and D. Callahan (eds), *Ethics in Hard Times*, Plenum, 1981.
21. Wolin, S.S., 'The American pluralist conception of politics', in A.L. Caplan and D. Callahan (eds), *Ethics in Hard Times*, Plenum, 1981.
22. Parsons, T. and Shils, E., *Towards a General Theory of Action*, Harvard University Press, 1951.
23. Mumford, E., *Values Technology and Work*, Martinus Nijhoff, 1981.

3 Systems design in an unstable environment

This chapter considers the changes in employment contracts and the deterioration in employer-employee relationships in recent years. It asks if an ethical approach which takes account of staff needs and interests can reverse the present unsatisfactory situation. It discusses the role that a humanistic systems designer might play in this reversal.

Organizational perspectives

Organizations can be studied from many different angles and perspectives [1]. There is a mechanistic point of view, in which they are seen as the instruments of their owners, with efficiency, reliability and predictability as their main functions. The organization is now viewed as a machine, with technology as its principal facilitator. This perspective has its own critical literature, with writers such as Zygment Bauman warning of the risks ahead as technology removes one set of problems, while replacing them with another containing greater risks and more unknown consequences [2].

A second perspective is the organismic view in which organizations are seen as living systems with functions but without purposes, other than survival. This was discussed in the last chapter in the section on what could be learnt from biology.

The third perspective is the social systems view that defines organizations as voluntary associations of purposeful members. Such systems enable ethical choices to be made concerning both ends and means; what to do and how to do it. With this definition the purpose of an organization is to serve the interests of its members, both employees and shareholders. It does this by meeting the needs of its environment – customers, suppliers and associated groups.

As this book is about ethical choice, the social system perspective is the one that fits best. It enables us to focus on social relationships and management philosophies. For example, organizations that try to serve their members will want to reduce dysfunctional conflict. Creative conflict can be an invigorating and stimulating force, but negative conflict, with different groups fighting each other, can be destabilizing and expensive. Conflict of this kind can occur as a result of a clash of personalities, but more often it arises because of adverse factors in the environment which put pressure on internal groups. These problems may restrict choice by forcing strategies directed at survival on a company, or they may only offer choices between a number of unpopular and morale-reducing changes.

This chapter examines some of the changes that have been and are taking place in companies as a result of the recent recession and alterations in the structure of world trade. Many of these are seen as worsening the quality of working life for staff, with stress being substituted for job satisfaction. They can all present dilemmas for the systems designer or manager who supports people-centred values and continuing good human relationships.

The question that this chapter raises is 'How possible is it to make ethical choices in unstable, even hostile, environments?' It argues that while it may be very difficult to accomplish desired change, in order to appreciate what is possible the systems designer who acts as a change agent must understand what is taking place in the environment and how this affects relationships between management, employees, suppliers and customers. To assist this understanding, we will look again at each contract described in the last chapter, examine what has happened to it and suggest ethical strategies for reducing conflict and improving human relations. We will also suggest how a systems designer might respond to these strategies.

Promises of the past

In 1908 a banker, Henry Clewes, gave some fatherly advice to the students at Yale. He said:

> *Survival of the Fittest:* You may start in business, or the professions, with your feet on the bottom rung of the ladder; it rests with you to acquire the strength to climb to the top. You can do so if you have the will and the force to back you. There is always plenty of room at the top .... Success comes to the man who tries to compel success to yield to him. Cassius spoke well to Brutus when he said, 'The fault is not in our stars, dear Brutus, that we are underlings, but in our natures' [3].

Here was a description of the Protestant Ethic in its purest form. Today, after years of spreading bureaucracy and increased government interference, we seem to be back there again, locked into a value system of 'competitive individualism'. The value system of the 1990s has encouraged a belief in the importance of competition and the need for high performance to achieve the desired 'competitive edge'. We are told that the holy grail can only be reached through revolutionary change in which old ideas and practices are abandoned and new, more efficient and ruthless ones, are substituted.

But today's problem is that this capitalist Utopia is not sought only by a few, as it was at the turn of the century. Now, everyone wants to be winners with the result that there is a growing mismatch between aspirations and economic reality. Added to this there are major changes in company structures with outsourcing, downsizing and re-engineering all taking place. These have produced redundancies which have affected the middle classes as well as the working class.

These changes have caused a transformation of Galbraith's contented classes into an anxious and resentful group. A rich society has become a demoralized and neurotic society.

Professor Peter Townsend, writing in the *British Medical Journal*, has described how economic changes are producing new attitudes to wealth and to the responsibility it brings. These evoke memories of the early days of the industrial revolution – before the Protestant Ethic had taken hold and the welfare state had been established [4]. Praise is given to extreme individualism, while deregulation, cuts in public spending, control of trade unions and local authorities, and privatization are regarded as beneficial and desirable. He points out that this widening inequality must create social problems. In his view, the 'culture of contentment' among the prosperous induces a politics of vindictiveness and selfish complacency. He warns that 'no evidence exists that charitable, still less egalitarian, motives come to the fore.'

Cultural influences

In Europe, at present, American business schools appear to exert an unduly powerful influence on management expectations and behaviour by 'hyping' old and new ideas such as 'total quality', 'business process re-engineering', 'core competencies', 'competitive edge' and other emotive terms. These ideas are then actively marketed by European consultants anxious to acquire new business. Many companies respond by introducing major change programmes associated with these apparent panaceas. Some of these work well, others do not; but the fact that a considerable number result in redundancies lowers morale, reduces security and causes resistance to change.

This upheaval can have a major impact on the employer–employee contract. Conservative companies tend to employ conservative workers who want stability and security rather than risk and excitement. Yet many of our most conservative companies – banks and insurance firms, for example – have succumbed to the competitive pressures, have jumped on the cost cutting bandwagon, and are offering their employees the unwanted challenge of early retirement, performance related pay, part-time work and short-term contracts. All of these generate uncertainty and low morale.

A survey of British companies with 200 to 5000 employees in 1992 found that 88% of the responding organizations (16.2% of the sample replied) had experienced job loss situations with enforced redundancies. Over 46% perceived decreased motivation in those who remained [5].

Redundancies can be traumatic for everyone. Those who have to leave are subjected to considerable stress, but those who stay can also be affected, with anxiety upsetting both staff and customer relationships [6]. Research has shown that this instability can cause a 'survivor guilt syndrome'. People feel guilty that they still have a job while their friends have lost theirs. The result can be antagonism towards management and fear of the future. Psychologists tell us that feelings of guilt stem from depression. When people find themselves in situations over which they have no control, which could affect them, and which have damaging consequences, they feel hopeless and helpless, have low self-esteem and transfer feelings of criticism and guilt to themselves [7].

Those who retain their jobs seem to be working much longer hours to make up for staff reductions. This is particularly true in the United States where employees work 320 more hours a year than their European counterparts. In Britain, which now has the longest working hours in Europe, teachers, medical staff, lawyers and even the clergy all have the same problem. The reason for this is a desire to compete more effectively by reducing unit costs. This, despite its consequences for morale, is called achieving greater efficiency.

Women may be particularly adversely affected by the present situation. Their family responsibilities mean that it is not always possible for them to work long hours. The equality group, Opportunity 2000, says that its campaign to persuade companies to introduce 'family-friendly' policies is incompatible with the obsession of many companies to reduce their 'head count'. Although the campaign to promote more women in the workplace enjoys the ministerial support, tough management policies are making progress very difficult.

Technology is another catalyst for change that can have mixed results and affect company attitudes. Good systems, carefully introduced, can bring major benefits. Poor, or inappropriate, systems badly introduced can cause drops in morale, increased costs and periods of business uncertainty. The British health service, in particular, has suffered from a number of large, expensive projects which have failed to deliver what was promised.

The futurologist, Alvin Toffler, predicts that the information revolution is making many of our old assumptions about industrial culture obsolete. He speaks approvingly of a future which is decentralized, niche-marketed and based on a 'just-in-time' philosophy. The question is 'Is this what we want?' Do we want a rapidly accelerating bandwagon from which many people fall off, or do we want a slower moving, more stable society which cares for the poor, sick and old and is prepared to lower its economic demands for greater social benefits? A Canadian academic, Arthur Kroker, has pointed out that technology can work in two ways. It can speed things up, but it can also slow things down. He suggests that we need to work towards the *recline* of western civilization rather than the *decline*. We need to lower our aspirations for wealth and settle for greater equality and a slower, better balanced and more comfortable existence [8].

The contracts of the 1990s

Given these pressures, let us examine how the nature of the work contracts is changing in the 1990s.

THE KNOWLEDGE CONTRACT

This contract is based on the agreement between the employer and the employee that the employee will provide the skills and knowledge required by the employer while, in return, the employer uses and pays for these and helps the employee to develop them further.

In early studies by the author this contract was poor for employees at lower levels in most companies. Clerical workers complained that their work was routine and boring and that their skills were not developed. Employers, in contrast were quite satisfied with the situation unless they suffered from skill shortages. These were generally overcome by offers of higher pay to employees with the required skills in competing companies.

Today, the nature of this contract has altered. The requirement now is for a flexible labour force which is prepared to learn a variety of job skills and to move to new jobs at frequent intervals. The demand for a labour force willing to accept routine, unchallenging work has become much less. In Britain, unfortunately, despite government attempts at improvement, the training situation is little different from the past, with employers firing staff who cannot cope with the new jobs and again attracting new staff by offering higher pay than their competitors. Will Hutton points out that savage cuts in public spending on training, together with companies' own cutbacks, have made skilled workers more and more valuable [9].

The opportunities for skill development have become greater, but so has work pressure and job insecurity.

THE PSYCHOLOGICAL CONTRACT

This contract relates to the employer's need to have a loyal, enthusiastic and motivated labour force and the employee's wish for psychological rewards such as 'a sense of achievement', responsibility, recognition and opportunities for advancement [10].

At present the psychological contract seems to be experiencing considerable negative distortion and to have major contradictions located in it. Employees are expected to be loyal, and highly motivated to achieve quality and performance standards, while their long-term employment prospects are being eroded with stress substituted for job satisfaction. There is no longer confidence that employment will last for any length of time; redundancy could happen tomorrow. A leader in the *Independent On Sunday* newspaper of 1 January, 1995, was headed 'Welcome back Stakhanov'. It predicted: 'In 1995 many workers will be trying to emulate a soviet miner. In 1925 he mined 102 tons of coal in one shift, prompting a Soviet propaganda drive to encourage workers to exceed their production norms. We are all Stakhanovites now.' This de-layering and rationalization – the jargon words for putting people out of work – is changing the British culture. One solution would be to distribute available work among as many people as possible through an increase in part-timers. But this makes no sense to most employers. It is easier and cheaper to pile more and more work upon fewer and fewer individuals.

Fifteen years ago this situation would have provoked an angry reaction from the trades unions and, probably, some major strikes to force employers to behave more humanely. For the time being, this countervailing force is missing.

THE EFFICIENCY CONTRACT

This is the contract that now dominates work. Whereas, in the past, it covered providing services and technology that enabled the employee to work more efficiently in a comfortable environment, it now seems to focus almost entirely on the financial interest of the employer to reduce unit costs. Technology is speeding work up but it is also removing many jobs. At the same time we are entering an era of telework in which employees interact with each other from considerable physical distances. The problems of these new kinds of association are still virtually unknown.

Technology has always been a destabilizing force for employees. Today, it is only one destabilizing force among many in most industrial countries. In America employment is up and inflation down, which sounds good for everyone. But wages have not increased in line with inflation and people are being asked to work much harder. In the past ten years seventeen days have been added to the work year. Europe is not as far advanced in increasing demands on employees but Britain, in particular, seems to be following the American path. This can lead to a more demoralized, rather than a more efficient, labour force.

Today's managers do not boast of the quality of the work environment they offer their staff but of how many people they have fired, retired early or put on short-term contracts. Peter Wickens, for many years a director of the Japanese Nissan Corporation, warned the Institute of Personnel Development 1994 annual conference that managers are in danger of putting too much pressure on employees. He pointed out that many Japanese firms do not provide models that should be followed; on the contrary, they may offer what he described as 'a lousy quality of working life' [11].

THE WORK STRUCTURE CONTRACT

This used to be the focus of interest of groups such as the Tavistock Institute of Human Relations which argued that work should be designed to make it more interesting and challenging. Each individual could then achieve a satisfactory relationship with work and the work environment. Today, as we have seen, the problem appears to be not too much routine, but too much stress. New production philosophies, such as lean manufacturing with its 'just-in-time' philosophy have created very tight production systems in which the worker has to accomplish a great deal in a short period of time without making any errors. Peter Wickens believes that modern management techniques are causing problems for employees. He says: 'People should not become the casualties of the improvements they create.'

In theory this contract, together with the knowledge contract, would seem to be the areas which have improved in the new work climate. The efforts of many behavioural scientists in America and Europe in the 1950s, 1960s and 1970s were directed at ameliorating the slavery of arduous, boring jobs, such as those associated with the moving assembly line, and the tedious routine of many low level clerical jobs. The British Tavistock Institute was one of the pioneering groups most active in this campaign. Their early socio-technical model was directed at increasing the level and mix of skills that employees were able to develop in the work situation.

This problem of routine work is decreasing as technology takes over more jobs through computers and robotics. The humans working with these machines require higher grade skills, more knowledge and greater flexibility of response. This should be greatly to their benefit, but unfortunately this situation also contains a number of contradictions. Managers want employees to be flexible and skilled while, at the same time, they try to exert tighter control through appraisal schemes and work measurement. Managers require a highly motivated workforce while offering the negative motivators of loss of job through redundancy, dismissal or non-renewal of contract.

The employees best able to resist these pressures are those who still possess strong unions; for example, doctors, teachers and railwaymen.

THE VALUE CONTRACT

This last and most important contract sets out the ethical principles that each side wants or expects from the other. It covers intangibles such as mutual loyalty and trust, shared objectives and the provision of a high quality of working life for employees. Over the years many European firms have built their reputations on the strength of this contract. Its practical form has been shown in effective consultation, good communication, a continuing concern for the welfare of all employees, both in work and at home, and a wish to be seen as a good, caring employer, whose first responsibility is to employees rather than to shareholders.

In Britain, many firms today seem unable to accommodate these traditional values. The pressures of competition, recession and privatization, together with the greatly reduced strength of the trades unions, have enabled many managements to proceed almost unchallenged to the goal of reduced unit costs at any price. A question that needs to be answered is 'Why has there been so little challenge?'

C.H. Prahalad, another speaker at the 1994 conference of the Institute of Personnel and Development, asked the delegates 'How can you tell people that they are the most important resource when all they can see is that they are the most expendable resource?'

T. Keenoy, a lecturer at the Cardiff Business School in an article in *The Observer* newspaper describes today's paradoxes: the desire to motivate employees, while at the same time controlling them; the desire for total employee commitment, while offering only short-term contracts; the desire for flexibility and quality, while insisting on continual performance auditing; the carrot of economic reward with the stick of loss of job security [12].

Professor Cary Cooper warns us of the dangers ahead for society as well as industry. He points out 'Organizations are reducing their full-time permanent staff and are no longer taking on people for life. Instead we have people in short-term jobs, on contract, or working on particular projects. The trend is for these "contingency" workers, as they are called in the US, to be brought in for specific tasks and then that's it. It has all been happening so quickly that no-one has been asking what are the implications for health, for family life, or for the nature of organizational behaviour' [13].

The *Independent On Sunday* (18.12.94) repeats this warning [14]. Its correspondent, Ian Parker says:

> Work is making us nervous. We don't recognize the place. In Britain in 1994 people who do not have a job feel very bad, but people who do have a job feel almost equally bad. British workers are intimidated by recent, fairly sudden and probably irreversible changes in the labour market.

The question again is why has there been so little opposition to this threatening situation? Why have line managers not asked questions? What has happened to personnel managers, a group that used to pride themselves on their ability to look after the welfare of employees and act as mediators between workers and management? What, too, has happened to the trades unions? Has their power diminished to such an extent that they have been unable to make any useful response? It seems that the removal of their power, allied to unemployment, privatization and general world economics has created a bewildered and vulnerable labour force. Because the unions are unable to meet these challenges managers have proceeded virtually without restraint.

Changing the situation

Let us assume that our systems designer is working for a firm that has downsized and outsourced in an attempt to reduce its unit costs. But it has failed to become profitable and has been taken over by another company called People First. People First recognizes that it has acquired a company which can become profitable but in the meantime has a demoralized work force. It also believes strongly that the most important asset it has bought is the company employees. It now wants to reverse the employment practices of the previous owner and to provide a good work environment assisted by good new technology. It asks our systems designer to contribute to this new ethos.

People First believes that a majority of its employees are seeking stability. They want a work situation with a degree of predictability over which they have some control [15]. The new management has a theory that a successful organization is one that is

1. Capable of maintaining stability;
2. Able to change radically when necessary;
3. Able to decide the amount, direction and timing of its own change [16].

It wants employees who will welcome and handle both stability and change. It recognizes that different groups of employees will have different needs. The skilled may differ from the unskilled in what they regard as stability and acceptable change. Women may differ from men and the young may differ from the old.

People First decides that it needs to rethink and renegotiate the knowledge, psychological, efficiency, work structure and value contracts.

The knowledge contract

The firm recognized that work was becoming polarized. Yesterday's problem that work was generally being deskilled was no longer true but the trend was towards skill polarization [17]. Employees who had skills were finding that there were good opportunities to increase these, but employees with few skills were finding that they were losing those that they had. Generally, it was men rather than women who were the beneficiaries of this skill acquisition process, full-time rather than part-time workers, and the young rather than the old. In order to offset this trend People First decided to pay great attention to training. It believed that a highly trained and knowledgeable labour force would be an asset at all levels in the company.

It decided to rethink and adjust the knowledge contract in the firm. As a good employer it has always offered excellent skill training and knowledge development programmes to its staff. Success in these are rewarded by salary increases based on 'payment for knowledge', rather than the dubious 'payment for results'.

People First asked our systems designer if he would assist this change by avoiding the creation of very routine jobs when he designed new systems. It also asked him to supply a training specification and development programme for each old job that he changed and for each new job that he created. People First believed that this strategy would help to take care of present and future skill shortages and that everyone would gain from it. It found that employees were enthusiastic about the proposal. A majority wanted to learn more, for skill acquisition would bring them greater job opportunities and higher economic rewards. People First deplored the fact that in many firms training had become a victim of recession cost cutting. Its management believed that future economic success, as well as a more satisfied workforce, required skill training and knowledge development to become a management and government priority.

The psychological contract

People First regarded this as the contract where the divergence between employee needs and company needs had been greatest. The Herzberg motivators of recognition, responsibility, advancement and a sense of achievement seemed to have been removed from many jobs and departments. In their place had appeared the fear and insecurity of job loss [18]. Management agreed with Lord McCarthy, the British Labour Party's employment spokesman who, in the House of Lords, suggested that the new concepts of 'empowerment', 'downsizing' and 'flexibility' had all but destroyed notions of the decent employer, or of what constitutes 'good industrial relations'. Lord McCarthy said:

> In the past, such ideas were largely defined in terms of a stable and secure work environment, where management acted with consistency and justice. Worker notions of 'felt-fair' relationships between tasks and rewards were respected and observed by managers until they could be changed by consent. Now, all that can be expected, or permitted, is what can be afforded in terms of the external environment. The question is: can more applicable and reliant criteria for 'good industrial relations' be defined and applied to fit this product or customer-dominated climate?

For People First the answer was the creation of a work environment that created and maintained 'motivation'. Motivation in turn required mutual trust and responsibility. Employees needed to have confidence that in periods of necessary change they would be treated with care and consideration. Assurances must be given that every attempt would be made to soften the blow of redundancy, if this could not be avoided, and to control and reduce the stress for those who remained. This required honesty and openness from management. It also required strategies and procedures to prevent those who stayed and those who went from becoming the victims of situations over which they had no control.

Our systems designer recognized immediately that any system he introduced must be relevant, acceptable and motivating. He decided that asking users to participate in the design processes would be a good way of achieving this. He remembered that at university he had been recommended to read the papers of an American management expert called Mary Parker Follett. She was a contemporary of Frederick Winslow Taylor in the 1920s. He decided to read these again [19].

He found that she believed that a major contribution to organizational stability came from good coordination, and that this came about through effective communication and problem solving. She recommended four fundamental principles of organization. These were:

Coordination by direct contact
All employees must be in direct contact, regardless of their position in the organization. Horizontal communication is as important as vertical chains of command in achieving coordination. The systems designer made a note to let everyone know what was happening when he designed a new system, irrespective of whether they were involved or not.

Coordination in the early stages
Employees should be involved in policy or decisions while these are being formed and not simply brought in afterwards. In this way the benefits of participation will be obtained in increased motivation and morale. The systems designer decided: I must involve users in the design task as soon as possible, even asking the question 'Should we change or not?'

Coordination as the 'reciprocal relating' of all factors in a situation
All factors should be related to one another, and these interrelationships must themselves be taken into account. Systems designer: I must always try to think through the possible consequences of design decisions. Who will be affected and how.

Coordinating is a continuous process
An executive decision is a moment in a process. So many people contribute to the making of a decision that the concept of final or ultimate responsibility is an illusion. Combined knowledge and joint responsibility take its place. Authority and responsibility should derive from the actual function to be performed, not from place in the hierarchy. Systems designer: The participation process must be long term and continuous. All who will be affected by it must be consulted.

The efficiency contract

People First knew that in the firm it had taken over it was this contract that now dominated work. It was a tough, management structured, contract in which the firm set standards, introduced new technology and set wage and salary rates without any consultation or communication. It was also the contract which, in the past, the trades unions had had most influence on. Their ability to question strategy was now greatly reduced. A Theory X management of tight controls had replaced a Theory Y belief in autonomy and self-control [20].

People First wished to improve the efficiency contract by substituting a more 'caring' management style for the 'macho' management of the past. They believed this would lead to better relationships with staff and, because of this, to increased efficiency. But it required a change in management values. People First wished to create an environment for its staff that provided autonomy in work, opportunities for personal development, and the treatment of employees as partners rather than subordinates. It knew that, in the 1970s and 1980s, a considerable amount of American and European industry had introduced these ideas and accepted them as good management practice.

People First also wished to re-establish good relationships with its trades unions. It believed that these were rethinking their role, were anxious to abandon the old confrontational relationships and wanted to form a constructive partnership with firms that they regarded as good employers.

The systems designer recognized that these changes would have a big impact on his work. They would affect the systems he selected for implementation and the way he designed and introduced them. He too would have to support company values and adopt a more 'caring' approach. He was delighted to do this.

The work structure contract

Many employees in People First had found that their work had changed dramatically in recent years. Too much routine had generally been replaced by too much stress. Workers were increasingly required to be skilled and flexible, although at the same time they had been subjected to tight controls and exacting time and quality targets. This meant that the pressure of work had greatly increased. People First management now wanted, wherever possible, to find and implement tools, techniques and technology that were both efficient and humanistic. They knew of the Volvo experiments [21][22] with multi-skilled groups and believed that this approach was flexible, good for quality and motivating for employees. They would try to use it wherever it was economically viable.

The systems designer accepted that his challenge was to make a humanistic approach as efficient and economic as possible through the appropriate selection and use of new technology.

The value contract

People First believed that this was the most important of the five contracts, as it influenced all the others. It was concerned with the organizational climate of the company as a whole. If the new values were accepted, developed, implemented and approved by all employees and management, then many things would become possible. A problem here could be that the kinds of values most likely to be desired and accepted by employees, namely values related to their interests, would not necessarily be the values of management. Employees were concerned with economic rewards and with the quality of working life, while managers were concerned with profits and controls.

The question then became 'Is it possible to develop a set of values that both management and employees can accept?' With the new objectives of management these values must be humanistic if they were to act as a motivating force for employees. This led to a second, difficult question. Given that the firm still had some managers who had worked for the previous owners, how could they be persuaded to accept and adopt these kinds of values? They had to be shown that humanistic values were, in the long term, more profitable than technical or economic values on their own. They believed that American experience could help them here. Some US experts were now arguing for what they call enlightened 'collective' strategies rather than corporate strategies. All employees should share an aspiration for the enterprise and possess a clear sense of the legacy that they were trying to build [23].

Another expert, Tom Peters, in one of his influential books [24], had stressed the importance of leadership, saying:

> The leader's main role is to add coherence to a real but ambiguous world. That only happens when the boss hangs out, observes – and then explains, vividly, what he or she has seen and what it means in the scheme of things.

The systems designer was beginning to realize that to achieve humanistic values in industry required leadership, vision, bravery and risk-taking. It also required consensus – the recognition by all that the preferred values are in everyone's best interests and should be implemented and maintained. He remembered that Mary Parker Follett had written:

> Morality is never static; it advances as life advances.... The true test of morality is not the rigidity with which we adhere to standards, but the loyalty we show to the life that constructs standards. The test of our morality is whether we are living not to follow but to create ideals, whether we are pouring our life into our visions, only to receive it back with its miraculous enhancement for new uses [25].

He had also recently read a position paper produced by the Institute of Personnel and Development which gave some good advice on how to implement and reinforce desired values [26]. It suggested:

- Values need to be relevant and understandable. Unless they relate to mission and/or vision statements they may undermine them.
- Top team training will be necessary to make sure that top managers understand the values of the organization and their influence, to enable them to act in ways which are consistent with the values.
- Inappropriate alternative values may be created if there is incompatibility between stated values and standards and management action.
- It will be more difficult in the future to develop trust if fewer people are working in full-time jobs on indefinite contracts.

Sir Richard Greenbury, the Chairman of Marks & Spencer, when he received the British Quality of Management award had reinforced this by saying:

The most critical challenge facing us today is the development of the quality of people needed to manage an increasingly large and complex international business. Our consistent growth and success has largely been due to our meeting this challenge.

The systems designer of People First realized that he must rethink his role.

The new role of the systems designer

The People First systems designer decided that in order to make an effective contribution he needed to become more multidisciplinary, participative and reflective. By reflective he meant thoughtful, insightful and able to learn from his experiences.

Greater multidisciplinary knowledge was required because he was operating in an increasingly complex world. Every design problem he was presented with was located in a concrete situation with many different needs and processes [27]. Many of these situations were dynamic because company business strategies were changing at the same time. Often these changes were unexpected and unanticipated as, for example, when senior management suddenly decided to create a new department. This meant that early system objectives had to be altered to take account of the new organization. Changes of this kind required rethinking of needs and policies, and could cause additional pressure. The system might have to be rethought, redesigned and require new implementation procedures. This kind of challenge was happening much more frequently than in the past.

The systems designer was convinced that he must broaden his knowledge base. In addition to skills in technical design he also needed a knowledge of psychology, sociology, communication, and strategies for managing change. Although he could never be an expert in these subjects, he must know enough to appreciate when he needed to call in an appropriate specialist.

It was also necessary for him to recognize the relevance of user participation to successful systems design. He must appreciate who the stakeholders were and get them interested, involved and committed. He must also try to see things from their point of view. Stakeholders would include both groups who provided the system with data and recipients of the information that the system provided. He recognized that design in complex environments needed to be a collective task. The knowledge of the user groups would be valuable inputs into the design process.

But he also believed that groups of this kind required a leader and hoped that he might be able to handle this role. As a leader, part of his responsibility would be to transfer as much of his knowledge as possible to the members of the supporting group.

Most importantly, he needed to become what Schon has called a 'reflective' manager – a manager who thinks a great deal about what he or she is doing [28]. He believed that as a systems designer he was on a voyage of discovery, constantly required to understand and handle new kinds of problems. This required him to try new approaches and perhaps take more risks. He must also persuade his colleagues that technical knowledge was no longer sufficient and that the broadening process must apply to them also. An important message to get across was that problems cannot be solved unless they are first understood.

He recognized that the skills of the multidisciplinary, participative, reflective systems designer were even more important when he or she was working in a difficult, demanding and unstable environment. Here, unanticipated changes were likely to be frequent and challenging events. Here, an understanding of the negative factors in the situation was of critical importance. It was as important to know what could not be done, as to understand what was possible. For example, user participation might not be well received if a new system was going to cause loss of jobs.

The most pressing problem now was to begin acquiring this additional knowledge. This would require study, discussions with experts, learning from the experience of other companies, and trying out new approaches. His goal was the following:

To be a technological leader, a man of knowledge who is able to cultivate and use this knowledge for the benefit of others. But, even more important, to be a social leader, someone who can help others to introduce and manage positive change without stress, disharmony or victims.

References

1. Gharajedaghi, J. and Geranmayeh, A. 'Performance criteria as a means of social integration' in J.M. Chouktown and R.M.Snow (eds), *Planning for Human Systems*, University of Pennsylvania Press, 1992.
2. Bauman, Z., *Post-modern Ethics*, Blackwell, 1993.
3. Whyte, W.H., *Organization Man*, Cape, 1957.
4. Townsend, P., 'The rich man in his castle' in *British Medical Journal* Vol. 309, 1674-1675, 1994.
5. Barrell, R. (ed.), *The UK Labour Market*, Cambridge University Press, NIESR, 1994).
6. Doherty, N. Tyson, S. and Viney, C., 'A positive policy? Corporate perspectives on redundancy and outplacement', *Personnel Review*, Vol.22, No. 7, 45-53, 1993.
7. Garber, J and Seligman, E.P., *Human Helplessness*, Academic Press, 1980.
8. Beard, S., 'The Futures Market', *The Observer Life Magazine*, 3.4.94.
9. Hutton, W., *The State We're In*, Cape, 1995.
10. Herzberg, F., *Work and the Nature of Man*, World Publishing, 1966.
11. Wickens, P., Speech to IPD Conference, Harrogate, 1994.
12. Keenoy,T., 'Performing Somersaults', *The Observer*, 18.9.94.
13. Cooper, C., *Times Higher Educational Supplement*, 30.12.94.
14. Parker, I., *The Observer*, 18.12.94.
15. Burnand, G., *Via Focal Problems*, Leadership Limited, 1982.
16. Gould, S.J., 'Is a new and general theory of evolution emerging?' in (ed. F.E.Yates), *Self-organizing Systems: The Emergence of order*, Plenum, 1987.
17. Braverman, H., *Labour and monopoly Capital*, Monthly Review Press, 1974.
18. McCarthy, Lord. Comment in *People Management*, 18.5.95.
19. Graham, P. (ed.) *Mary Parker Follett: Prophet of Management*, Harvard Business School Press, 1995.
20. McGregor, D., *The Human Side of Enterprise*, McGraw-Hill, 1960.
21. Lindholm, R. and Norstedt, J-P., *The Volvo Report*, Swedish Employers Association, 1975.
22. Berggren, C., *The Volvo Experience*, Macmillan, 1993.
23. Graham, P., op. cit.
24. Peters, T., *Liberation Management*, Macmillan, 1992.
25. Graham, P., op. cit.
26. Institute of Personnel Development, *People Make the Difference*, 1995.
23. Znanieck, F. *The Social Role of the Man of Knowledge*, Harper, 1968.
24. Schon, D., *The Reflective Practitioner*, Temple-Smith, 1983.

4 An ethical pioneer: Mary Parker Follett

This chapter discusses the ideas of Mary Parker Follett, an American administrator, who lectured and wrote in the 1920s and 1930s. Mary Parker Follett had revolutionary ideas on how employee involvement in problem solving and decision taking could be used to improve the efficiency and success of American industry. Mary Follett's ideas are compared with those of the human relations movement and with socio-technical design.

In the previous chapter we briefly discussed the ideas of Mary Parker Follett. We suggested that they might be relevant to a systems designer or change agent today, who wished to design new systems to improve the job satisfaction and quality of life for employees, as well as increase company efficiency. In this chapter her ideas are examined in more detail, as they are regarded as an ethical approach to the non-technical aspects of systems design. Mary Parker Follett believed that good consultation, and problem solving shared between management and the workforce, would lead to increased efficiency and business success.

The life of Mary Parker Follett

Mary Parker Follett was a highly educated woman. In 1890 she spent a year at Newnham College, Cambridge, England where she read political science, history and law. She followed this with six years at Radcliffe College, Cambridge, Massachusetts, graduating in 1898 after studying philosophy, economics and government. This led to further postgraduate study in Paris.

She regarded herself as a political scientist and her first major interest was the study of American public life. She contributed to the improvement of this by pioneering a network of evening classes for the young people of Boston, and in 1909 she produced her first important publication. This was called *The Speaker of the House of Representatives*. Prior to this publication, she had become interested in vocational guidance as a result of a visit to Edinburgh in 1902, where she had seen some pioneering work on this subject. In 1912 she became a member of the Boston Placement Committee which later became the Boston Department of Vocational Guidance. This took her into industry and she began researching working conditions in different sectors while, at the same time, she became increasingly interested in the problems of management and industrial relations.

In 1920 she produced her main work. This was called *The New State: group organization the solution of popular government*. It was published in London by Longman [1]. In this book she advocated the replacement of bureaucratic institutions by group networks in which the people themselves analyzed their problems and implemented their own solutions. This book was followed in 1924 by a second influential work called *The Creative Experience* [2]. In this she discussed the possibility of accepting and using conflict as a positive and enriching experience.

Mary Parker Follett was now famous as a political scientist. *The New State* was reviewed in journals throughout the world and brought her international recognition. It led to her becoming a friend of the British Lord Haldane and of many other distinguished philosophers and political scientists. But gradually, through her increasing contacts with industry, she moved away from political science and the problems of government to social administration and business management.

She gave many lectures to interested audiences. On visits to England in 1926 and 1928 she spoke at the Rowntree Lecture Conferences in Oxford and to the National Institute of Industrial Psychology. In 1929, after the death of the friend she lived with in Boston, she moved to England and stayed there until 1933.

While living in England she continued her studies of management, explaining to an audience at the London School of Economics that she did this

because industry is the most important field of human activity and management is the fundamental element in industry.

She died in December, 1933, when on a brief return visit to the United States.

During her early studies in the United States, Mary Parker Follett met Dr H. Metcalf and he later published many of her lectures. It was he, who together with a British management consultant, Colonel L. Urwick, in 1941 assembled her lectures in a book called *Dynamic Administration*. This was published in London by The Management Publications Trust. Many years ago the present author had the good fortune to secure a copy of this book. In the introduction the chocolate magnate and philanthropist B.S. Rowntree wrote:

The principles which she outlined are fundamental to all human progress. They should be widely known and acted upon, particularly at the present time, when good organization is of supreme importance to national survival. They will be found more necessary when the war is over and humanity is faced with the almost superhuman task of fashioning a new and better world [3].

But, despite her international fame Mary Parker Follett's writing and influence vanished from the American scene after her death. In a new book *Mary Parker Follett: Prophet of Management* edited by Pauline Graham, Peter Drucker in his introduction tries to find an explanation [4]. He describes how when, in 1941, he asked management experts to help him compile a reading list of important management books, no-one mentioned her name. It was when he met Colonel Urwick in 1951 that he first heard of her. Drucker claims that there was no reference to her in any American management book until he published his *Practice of Management* in 1954 [5]. Even here, when this author checked she found that the only reference there was the title *Dynamic Administration* in a selected bibliography. Follett did not appear in the index.

Drucker discounts the suggestion that she was neglected because she was a woman, claiming that there were many prestigious women around at the time, for example, Lilian Gilbreth, the wife of Frank Gilbreth and also a time and motion study expert. He argues that she was pushed into obscurity because her ideas were regarded as subversive in the 1930s and 1940s. Running industry after the Second World War was seen as a battle between management and unions. Her ideas on communication, conflict resolution and joint problem solving had no legitimacy. Contemporary management believed that the route to success was control not consensus. And so Mary Parker Follett became a non-person. She might never have existed. However, Rosabeth Moss Kantor who provides a preface to the new book does not agree with Drucker that there was no sexism in her rejection. She believes that Follett's gender did play an important part in her neglect.

Like many prophets who are neglected at home, her star continued to shine in other countries. The Japanese embraced many of her ideas and through Dr Metcalf and Colonel Urwick her work was kept alive in Britain. In the 1970s and 1980s many British books on organizational theory and management had chapters on Mary Parker Follett. All used the Metcalf and Urwick book as their information source.

The ideas of Mary Parker Follett

Mary Parker Follett had many highly innovative ideas and theories. First she believed that good human relationships required order. But order must be integral to the situation and must be recognized as such. Even though different groups with different interests would have different views, all should agree on the nature of the problems that had to be solved. Order should be the agreed 'law of the situation', but order and orders must be the composite conclusion of those who give and those who receive them. In her view industrial harmony comes from efforts to achieve consensus and from the efforts of the individual and the group, not the individual alone.

Mary Parker Follett took a holistic view of business and business organizations. She believed in integration. She tells us:

The first test of good business organization is whether you have a business with all its parts so coordinated, so moving together in their closely knit and adjusted activities, so linking, interlocking, interrelating, that they make a working unit – that is not a congeries of separate pieces [6].

Successful integration leads to good relationships because it encourages face-to-face communication, personalization and self assertion. It is not remote and bureaucratic. It takes account of the fact that situations are always evolving and that discussions and decisions must be circular and iterative, not linear.

In her view the undue influence of leaders is one of the main obstacles to integration. Orders and organization should not be a result of domination but come from a recognition by all parties of the problems that have to be tackled. Order and control then emerge from a common understanding and accepted 'law of the situation'.

Mary Parker recognized that freedom of action is often associated with power. The more power an individual has, the more he or she is likely to be free from constraints. She believed that what was required was not 'power over' but 'power with' or joint power. She says:

One of the tests of a conference or committee should be: are we developing joint power or is someone trying unduly to influence the others? [7].

In her view attempts must be made to reduce 'power over'. She asked:

How do we reduce power over? Individual freedom can lead to coercive exploitation. We want group freedom. Circular behaviour is the basis of integration. You influence another while they influence you. If both sides obey the law of the situation no person has power over another [8].

She continued:

Our first approach should always be to discover the law of the situation. We should try to reduce power over even if we cannot get rid of it.

She believed that power over could be reduced through integration, through recognizing that all should submit to the law of the situation and through making the business more and more of a functional unity. Function should equal capacity and there should be the authority and responsibility to go with the function.

When differences of opinion arise, she suggested that there are three ways of dealing with these – domination, compromise and integration. With domination only one side got what it wanted. With compromise neither side got what it wanted. But through integration it is possible to find a way in which both sides get what they want.

She pointed out that many think they are losing freedom and independence through joining with others but this is a false perception of freedom. Managers do not give up their freedom when they give their workers a share in management. On the contrary they are freeing themselves from strikes, sabotage and indifference. Employers are not free when these occur.

Mary Parker Follett translated these ideas from the individual firm to national and international level. She anticipated the Common Market by asking for the organization of markets:

> Nations cannot be free while struggling for markets. We want the organization of markets.

She saw no conflict between planning and freedom. In her view good planning could provide more freedom by creating opportunities for personal initiative.

> 'Individualism and collective control should equal collective self control.'

Mary Parker Follett saw effective relationships in work as problem solving and decision taking in which all played a part. To achieve this she developed the four fundamental principles of organization described in chapter 3 [9].
These were:

Coordination by direct contact
All employees must be in direct contact regardless of their position in the organization.

Coordination in the early stages
Employees should be involved in policy or decisions while these are being formed and not simply brought in afterwards.

Coordination as the 'reciprocal relating' of all factors in a situation
All factors should be related to one another, and these interrelationships must themselves be taken into account.

Coordinating is a continuous process
So many people contribute to the making of decision that the concept of final or ultimate responsibility is an illusion.

Mary Parker Follett accepted the traditional concepts of power, authority and leadership, but redefined these as 'power *with*', '*joint* responsibility' and '*multiple* leadership'.

She did, however, recognize that achieving this kind of harmony would not be easy. Problems that would have to be solved included facilitating communication between all interested groups. At a later date, Jürgen Habermas makes the same plea. Planning, whether local or national, has to be flexible enough to encourage initiative and experiment. Collective control and decentralized responsibility have to be made compatible. There is no place for regulation or coercion; everything should emerge from discussion and agreement.

Mary Parker Follett presents us with an ideal to strive for, even though it may be difficult to attain. She believed strongly in rational thinking, so that problems are fully understood, in effective planning and organization of a kind that is generally agreed, and in working through discussion and consensus.

Her definition of effective relationships is 'freedom for the individual and the group', with the one supporting and enhancing the other. This kind of freedom comes from knowledge, discussion and integration. It requires continuous and close communication, a recognition of common interests and a willingness to participate in solving problems. All conflicts can be solved, given an understanding of their nature and a desire for a solution. Goodwill and good relations are the route to freedom for all.

Related theories

This theoretical approach, although utopian, is not very different from Jürgen Habermas's theory of communicative action. This too is a theory of social interaction, with the objective of creating an 'ideal speech situation'. This is a situation in which there is undistorted communication with participants who are free and equal in their dialogue roles and can arrive at a rational consensus. This is in contrast to distorted forms of communication which are characterized by social domination, authoritarianism, etc. [10]. But, despite the similarity of their theories and despite living in the US during the Second World War, like Drucker, Habermas appears not to have heard of Follett.

All ideas have a past as well as a future, and Mary Parker Follett is no exception. She had studied political science and philosophy at Newnham and Radcliffe and in her early days she called herself a political scientist. It is most probable that her ideas were influenced by the thinking and writing of a number of classical philosophers, although we can only guess at which. Like her, many have taken as their point of departure the premise of an underlying unity and symmetry that could be uncovered through reason. William James called the proponents of these ideas the 'tender minded'. Some, including Aristotle, favoured the decentralization of authority and the encouragement of pluralism with many different interest groups. The sixteenth century philosopher Althusius believed in a community of communities, as did more recent thinkers such as Burke, Weber and Durkheim.

All of these saw freedom associated with function. Each group or community within the larger community should have the greatest possible autonomy, consistent with the performance of its function and with the performance of other groups and communities that it associated with. The emphasis of these philosophers was on the small and the local – the family, neighbourhood, local association and work group.

Edmund Burke in the eighteenth century detested what he called 'arbitrary power'. He saw society as a contract, or partnership founded on kinship, neighbourhood or social group. Hegel too in the nineteenth century viewed society as plural with many centres of authority. These included the church, local community, profession and occupational association. He describes freedom as 'being with oneself in another', that is, actively relating to something other than oneself in such a way that this other becomes integrated into one's projects, completing and fulfilling them so that it counts as belonging to one's own action. This means that freedom is possible only to the extent that we act rationally, and in circumstances where the objects of our action are in harmony with our reason [11].

Alexis de Tocqueville, the nineteenth century French philosopher, carried on the intellectual pursuit of democratic communities in which all men are equal. Pluralism had now taken a number of different forms. There was 'conservative' pluralism that saw its mission as the reinforcement of traditional groups, such as the family and the church. There was also 'liberal' pluralism which was concerned with the relationships between a democratic state and a structure of social organization that provided the highest degree of individual freedom. And there was 'radical' pluralism which was Marxist in inspiration and envisaged a totally new society.

Mary Parker Follett appears to fit in the tradition of 'liberal' pluralism which aims to provide individual freedom within the context of group freedom. She restricted her philosophy to the business organization, although she thought the principles could also be applied to national and international trade. If she lived in Britain today she would probably be a supporter of the Liberal Democrat party.

What is the situation today?

Daniel Bell has argued for a recognition of the complexity and variety of modern society. He sees Western industrial society as divided into different sectors, each guided by its own principle. There is the technoeconomy, whose guiding principle is efficiency; the political sphere, whose legitimacy is based on the concept of free and equal citizens; and the culture, increasingly dominated by the ideal of unlimited self-expression. Bell suggests that these apparently incompatible realms of society are a source of many of today's conflicts [12]. Can people who want self-development and fulfilment achieve this in an industrial society where roles and specialization still rule to a high degree? Will today's movement towards flatter hierarchies, multi-skilling, total quality and re-engineering bring the freedom and power-sharing that Mary Parker Follett desired, or are these new names for old bureaucracies?

For most of us a high quality of working life today means the capacity for choice and its exercise, the absence of constraining conditions and the availability of resources. It means equal opportunity for self-development in association with one's fellows, enabling conditions and the encouragement and motivation to take this route [13]. Self-development involves the creation of new capacities and the enrichment of existing ones – in other words a general enhancement in the quality of individual, group and organizational life [14]. Mary Parker Follett would be in agreement with all of these things.

But individualism and diversity for all require some generally agreed values. For example, an acceptance of the work ethic which requires personal independence to be associated with the desire to do a job well, and a restriction on untrammelled self-indulgence, so that the needs of the group are in harmony with the needs of the individual.

Who has followed Follett?

How close have we come to achieving these things? Have there been any serious and successful moves towards the kind of harmony that she strove for? The answer to this question is 'yes', although progress has been patchy, sporadic and, up to now, not greatly influenced by technology.

Human relations

The American 'human relations' movement of the 1950s, 1960s and 1970s had many ideas similar to those of Follett, although there is no acknowledgement of her in their writings. Elton Mayo was the founding father of the human relations school of thought and his experiments in the Hawthorne plant of the Western Electric Company made industry more aware of the fact that workers and managers must first be understood as human beings [15]. Frederick Herzberg, Chris Argyris, Rensis Likert and Douglas McGregor all followed in his footsteps. Frederick Herzberg spoke for them all when he said:

> The primary function of any organization, whether religious, political or industrial, should be to implement the needs of men to enjoy a meaningful existence [16].

Elton Mayo found that workers who were consulted, given responsibility for choosing their pace of work, and treated as partners rather than subordinates, responded with high motivation and high production. Mayo came to believe that an important task for management was to create situations where this spontaneous cooperation could develop and grow [17].

Chris Argyris's objective was to help people to attain satisfaction in work through developing their potential. He believed that this kind of self-actualization benefits not only the individual but also those around, as well as the employing organization. Again, better communication is a means for achieving this. Managers must be prepared to show their real feelings to those above and below them [18]. Herzberg too was interested in assisting the development of human potential. In his view job satisfaction came, not from money alone, but from achievement, recognition and responsibility. Jobs must be 'enriched' to provide these motivating factors [19].

Rensis Likert and Douglas McGregor had similar philosophies. Supervisors must be 'employee centred' and able to build effective work groups which have high achievement goals. They must regard their jobs as dealing with human beings rather than with work. Their role is to 'help' people to work efficiently, to exercise general but not detailed supervision and to allow maximum participation in decision taking. Likert's System 4 participative group management approach would also have delighted Mary Parker Follett. Communication now flows downwards, upwards and sideways; workers and bosses are psychologically close, decision taking is through group processes with each group linking to the next through a 'linking pin' individual who is a member of more than one group.

Likert was an admirer of Mary Parker Follett and her notion of 'the law of the situation'. He believed that the greater amount of objective information available to modern management enabled problems to be depersonalized and dealt with rationally and participatively [20].

Douglas McGregor followed on from these ideas with his Theory X and Theory Y management. Theory X is control and coercion, Theory Y is the development of 'supportive' relationships that enable employees to have self-actualization, responsibility, self direction and self-control [21].

A considerable amount of American industry responded to these ideas and they were increasingly accepted as good management practice. They were seen as enabling the needs and objectives of the individual and of the company to come together in a harmonious relationship. This was exactly what Mary Parker Follett had wanted to achieve.

Socio-technical systems

Europe did not have a human relations movement. In England, for example, management and workers looked at each other across a big divide, with each side regarding the other as 'the enemy'. The workers were usually backed by strong trades unions and the climate was more like a war game than a series of supportive relationships. But there were some new groups with ideas similar to those of Mary Parker Follett. One of the strongest of these was the socio-technical movement which emerged from the ideas of Eric Trist and the Tavistock Institute from the 1950s onwards [22][23].

Interestingly, although the Tavistock group came together soon after *Dynamic Administration* was published and although from its inception the ideas of the group have been close to those of Follett, there is no reference to her in the socio-technical literature.

Whereas the Americans focused on changing attitudes the British, and later European, groups believed that the answer to organizational health lay in the new forms of work structure that would improve efficiency but also create a good quality work environment and high job satisfaction. These new work structures were based on logically connected groups of tasks that enabled employees to acquire a number of skills, to do a whole job, to take decisions and to solve problems. They would also offer opportunities for working as members of integrated teams, for supportive relationships and personal development. Many of these ideas came from biology and from the notion of 'open' systems [24].

Early experiments with these semi-autonomous group structures were first carried out in the British Coal Industry and then moved to India, Scandinavia and the United States. Socio-technical design is still flourishing, although its scope and influence seem not to be known to the new proponents of business process re-engineering. It has a sound theoretical basis and a well-tested methodology. It takes a process and open system perspective, recognizing the dependencies between different parts of the work situation and between the work situation and the external environment.

The present author is now a Council member of the Tavistock Institute and so is closely in touch with its philosophy and approach. She first came into contact with it when she was asked to join the International Quality of Working Life Committee which consisted of STS practitioners from different parts of the world. Powerful figures at the time were Lou Davis in the United States, Hans Van Beinum in Canada, Federico Buttero in Italy, Einar Thorsrud in Norway, Fred Emery in Australia and, of course, the person who started it all, Eric Trist, who later moved to the United States and became a professor at the Wharton School. Although the STS pioneers were interested in both theory and practice Mary Parker Follett was never a subject for discussion. One reason for this may have been that the early interest in STS came principally from Scandinavia. With the exception of Professor Lou Davis at UCLA and one or two others socio-technical design in the US was slow to start.

The author's experience

The present author became interested in, and aware of, the ideas of Mary Parker Follett in the 1960s when she was fortunate enough to acquire a copy of *Dynamic Administration*. In the 1970s she became a member of the International Committee for the Quality of Working Life. Since then she has tried to apply the philosophies and principles of both Mary Parker Follett and socio-technical systems design. One of her objectives has always been to increase the user group's freedom to choose the organizational and technical system that they preferred. She has done this by using participative approaches which, whenever possible, involved all affected users in the design process.

She began to do this in the early 1970s when she was asked by different companies to help groups of staff to design and implement new computer systems. These groups were not computer specialists. They were often clerks who participated in the systems design task by identifying their information needs, choosing the best system to fit these needs and designing an effective organization of work around the new technology. Usually, the selected new form of work organization included important socio-technical design principles [25].

This early work in firms such as ICI, Rolls-Royce and many banks tried to achieve the socio-technical objective of optimal use of both technology and people, with employees being given the Follett freedom to analyze their own problems and agree and implement acceptable and viable solutions. In this way they could exert some influence on their future working conditions [26]. Humanistic technology was a desired output, but technology was not used to assist the design process.

This changed in the 1980s when the author undertook a large project with the Digital Equipment Corporation in Boston to assist the design of XSEL, one of Digital's first expert systems [27]. XSEL was a configuring aid directed at helping the Digital sales force to make fewer errors when they prepared financial estimates for customers and sent orders to the manufacturing plants. These errors were expensive and cost Digital a great deal of money through lawsuits and compensation payments.

Because XSEL was intended for all sales offices throughout the world and because the sales force were a powerful group, it was decided that the expert system must be designed participatively with the active involvement of the sales force. Digital believed that if the sales force where not given the freedom to do this they would respond by refusing to use the system. Freedom now was a necessity rather than an ideal.

The problem was how to do this when the sales force was so large. The answer was a representative design group of sales people, together with the use of electronic mail. An iterative design approach was used with the sales force specifying their needs, the knowledge engineers building a prototype to this specification and the sales force testing this out and commenting on their experience. This specify, build and test process continued until a system good enough to release for general use was produced. This took about three years.

During this period there were regular meetings of the design group and after each meeting an account of what had taken place was sent to each US sales office for discussion and comment. If questions were raised at the meeting that could not be easily answered, or decisions were difficult to make, the sales office staff were asked to send their views to the design group by e-mail. In this way a continuing dialogue concerning the design and implementation of XSEL took place. Through the use of e-mail, all sales staff could participate in this until the system became operational. Here then was a real world attempt at Mary Parker Follett's integrated communication using a new electronic aid.

Discussion of the technical quality of XSEL was also assisted by building a comments facility into the machine. Salespeople could use this to express their approval or dismay as they tested the system.

XSEL was implemented throughout the United States and worked fairly successfully for a number of years. The design group and the use of e-mail for communication continued during this period. This assisted the solution of technical problems and guided further development of the system.

Designing to assist harmony

If we accept that Mary Parker Follett's ideas are ethically and practically of value, what can we do about it? One thing we can do is to try to implement her ideas in the groups with which we work closely. If we are systems designers or other kinds of computer specialist we will be in constant touch with users. Here is the opportunity for a new approach with a humanistic and moral content.

The author explained earlier that she tried to use the philosophy of Mary Parker Follett and the objectives of the socio-technical school when helping users to design new systems. This is true whether these users are clerks, specialist groups or senior managers.

Here are some of principles that she finds most useful and relevant in her areas of activity.

Principles derived mainly from Mary Parker Follett

Participation
Users are always given a major role in the design process so that they can play an important part in the selection and design of systems that will improve their own efficiency, effectiveness, job satisfaction and quality of working life.

Giving users the freedom to take on this role enables them to have some control over the degree of freedom they can exercise in their new work situations.

Representation
All user interests need to be represented in a design group, irrespective of status, age or gender. Direct users of the new system should play a major role in systems design; indirect users should be consulted whenever factors that affect them are discussed.

Joint problem solving

Once the design group is operational, the first step is to get agreement on the problems and needs that have to be addressed through change. This is coming to a consensus on the 'Law of the Situation' – the nature of the problem that had to be solved. The group must agree that during meetings everyone is regarded as of equal status. The views of a junior clerk must be given as much weight as those of a senior manager. No single individual must be allowed to dominate the meeting. This point is particularly applicable to the technical specialists who may have favourite technical solutions that they want to press on to the participants.

Freedom of speech

There must be face-to-face communication, honest exchange of views and freedom of speech. Following Mary Parker Follett's advice, differences of opinion should be dealt with through integration, rather than domination or compromise. By integration is meant striving to achieve a 'win, win' solution. This is a solution from which all parties with a major interest in the new system feel that they have gained something.

Gaining power

The design group must recognize that by working together to ensure agreement on needs and solutions they can gain considerable power. They may need this power to ensure that their preferred solution is accepted by other powerful groups in the company. There needs to be a recognition that power is being increased, not lost, through the participation process. The technologists must believe that they are not losing power by sharing design with users. Senior management also must feel that they are not losing power by allowing lower level groups to take decisions. The accepted view should be that all are gaining power as good, well conceived systems are introduced that users want, understand and own.

Integrating all factors

The design group must also take account of all relevant factors in the situation that they want to change. It is not unusual for design groups to identify benefits and forget about costs. For example, a system that reduces staff numbers can greatly reduce costs, but this reduction may be offset by the costs of overworked and over-stressed staff who take time off from work because they cannot manage the additional work-load.

Staying together
The design group may wish to continue working together over a considerable period of time and this can have advantages. The XSEL design group met over many years, handling first the design process, next implementation and evaluation and, lastly, planning for the future development of XSEL.

Principles derived mainly from socio-technical design

Quality of working life
The most important principle is that an improvement in user quality of working life should be given as much importance as an improvement in efficiency.

Multi-skilling
Every effort should be made to design interesting, challenging and significant jobs for individuals and groups. However, challenge should not create high levels of stress.

Boundary management
All new designs, whether associated with hierarchies or processes, will include the movement across boundaries. As most serious problems occur on the boundary between one group or activity and another, careful attention must be paid to designing for good boundary management.

Information flow
Information systems should be designed so that information goes directly to the place where action is to be taken or to the source that originated it.

Continuing design
It must be recognized that the design task is never completed. It is a continuous, ongoing process.

Are Follett's ideas relevant today?

Today's management gurus are arguing forcibly that hierarchical and functional organizations are no longer working and will not work in the fiercely competitive world of the future [28]. They emphasize the need for change to improve efficiency and recommend panaceas such as business process re-engineering, total quality, performance-related pay and short-term contracts. They also stress the importance of information technology as a means for stimulating and ensuring the success of this kind of change.

But this is still an engineering view of the world. In 1903 Frederick Winslow Taylor was recommending a not-too-dissimilar kind of approach [29]. He wanted the optimum use of machines, a narrow division of labour, tight work standards and individual pay incentives. Yet people are the most important input to business success, and few of these new and old remedies pay much attention to their needs for participation, motivation, job satisfaction and creativity.

Mary Parker Follett saw the achievement of business success coming as much from enabling the individual and the group to contribute their skills and knowledge freely and without constraints. This kind of freedom came from motivated individuals, working together in small group situations within a close and integrated work environment. We now have to ask the question 'How relevant are her ideas today?' Can we still apply them in work situations where face-to-face communication is replaced or enhanced by video-conferencing, voice mail and telework, and where electronic networks are expanding to engulf every type of industrial and commercial activity.

First, let us remind ourselves of the ideas of Mary Parker Follett. She wanted freedom and responsibility for the individual and the group. This required group membership, communication, participation, joint problem solving and joint decision making. All of these have to take place both within groups and between groups. She believed in power and control but it was 'power with' not 'power over'. Power sharing of this kind requires common values and agreement on the cause and nature of problems. As already mentioned, this she called 'the Law of the Situation'. She also believed in multiple leadership so that no single individual or group was able to dominate the others. Similar ideas are still being propagated. In England, a distinguished social scientist, Geoffrey Vickers has written:

> We must abandon the idea that political and economic life is primarily the interaction of individuals, each pursuing their own self-interest.... We shall have to conceive ourselves as maintaining a number of institutional systems which are essential to our significance and survival, but which depend completely on our capacity to resolve or contain the conflicts which they engender.... This requires intelligence, tolerance, wisdom, acceptance of common constraints and assurances of membership [30].

Vickers believed that organizations can only survive if they are able to contain and resolve their conflicts and that communication and debate make a major contribution to this resolution. These provide a shared view of the problem and an understanding of each of the parties' special interests.

Charles Handy, another influential British writer on management supports this view, saying:

If we want to reconcile our humanity with our economics, we have to find a way to give more influence to what is personal and local, so that we each can feel that we have a chance to make a difference, that we matter, along with those around us.... A formal democracy will not be enough. We have to find another way, by changing the structure of our institutions to give more power to the small and to the local... [31].

Handy sees the answer in what he calls 'federalism'. Federalism is an old idea which had as one of its objectives the creation of a balance of power within an institution. Federal organizations are both small and large. They aim to be small and local in their appearance and in many of their decisions, but national, even global, in their scope. Like the Chinese philosophy of Yin and Yang they are built on contradictions. They endeavour to maximize independence while maintaining a degree of interdependence. Also, like Yin and Yang the secret of doing this successfully is achieving the right balance for the organization and the situation between things big and small. Individuals recognize and accept that they are members of both groups and that control is a shared activity.

Handy associates federalism with what he calls 'subsidiarity'. The individual parts retain as much independence as they can handle, but give some power to the centre because they know that the centre can do some things better. The centre is not necessarily large; it may be quite small, but it has a view of the whole. Today, this view is assisted by communications technology which provides it with the information it needs to survey the whole. Handy points out that subsidiarity is not empowerment. Empowerment implies that someone is giving away power. Subsidiarity means that power belongs lower down where most of the action takes place.

This form of organization requires small units with real power. The members of each unit are constantly in touch with other units, recognize and accept common rights and duties, and work together in a climate of mutual trust. Handy points out:

Organizations are nothing if they are not communities of people.... A community has members, not employees, and it belongs to its members [32].

Problems with these concepts

One problem is that they are very hard to achieve. Handy admits that the 'federal organization' is messy, untidy and always a little out of control. Nevertheless, he says, 'there is no real alternative in a complicated world.'

An important factor that can be an enhancer or reducer of harmony is current attitudes. Handy believes that human progress, as defined by Mary Parker Follett, is at present inhibited by our pursuit of efficiency and economic growth

So what is the end?

in the conviction that these are the necessary ingredients of progress. He believes that efficiency, like technology, should be a means, not an end in itself.

Technology is, of course, another factor that can reduce or increase the quality of working life. The history of technology is that its consequences have always been mixed. The more powerful have usually gained from its use, while the weaker have lost. One early group of sufferers were women clerks who found that they had lost what was often quite interesting manual work and become data input operators. This new job required concentration, was deadly boring and, to add insult to injury, the speed at which the women worked could be monitored by the computer and reported to management [33].

A group who constantly come under attack for causing technology to dehumanize work are the engineers. They are seen to be disciples of Taylor and, by writers such as David Noble, to be tools of the capitalist system using technology to reduce the human being to a machine component [34].

Hopefully, we have now passed this stage and the versatile computer is being used to enhance, not degrade, skills. Vickers points out that technology always makes ethical demands in what it requires people to expect of each other and therefore of themselves. In many fields today, the effect of technology is very positive, for the computer is an instrument of great variety that can be used in many different ways.

Let us hope this is true in its communication role, where it may help us to realize the democratic organization sought by Mary Parker Follett. Computers and networks can help us to communicate with people located far away, to take decisions based on accurate knowledge, to plan strategies with the alternatives clarified, to write joint papers and reports, and to pass around innovative ideas.

Blogs & Wikis

In theory this is splendid. The question is, will it work in the desired and desirable way? We are only just learning how to handle this new telefreedom and beginning to realize that the desired results are not so easy to achieve.

Mary Parker Follett's ideas give us something to aim for and provide a vision that many see as relevant for today's and tomorrow's urgent problems.

References

1. Follett, M.P., *The New State*, Longman, 1920.
2. Follett, M.P., *Creative Experience*, Longman, 1924.
3. Metcalf, H.C. and Urwick, L., *Dynamic Administration*, Management Publications Trust, 1941.
4. Graham, P., *Mary Parker Follett: Prophet of Management*, Harvard Business School Press, 1994.
5. Drucker, P.F., *The Practice of Management*, Harper, 1954.
6. Follett, M.P., 'The psychological foundations of business administration' in (ed. H.C. Metcalf) *The Scientific Foundations of Business Administration*, Williams and Wilkins, 1926.

7. Ibid.
8. Ibid.
9. Pugh, D.S., Hickson, D.J. and Hinings, C.R., *Writers in Organizations*, Penguin, 1971.
10. Gould,C., *Rethinking Democracy*, Cambridge University Press, 1988.
11. Wood, A.W., *Hegel*, Cambridge University Press, 1991.
12. Bell, D., *The Coming of a Post-Industrial Society*, Heinemann, 1974.
13. Galston, W.A., *Liberal Progress*, Cambridge University Press, 1991.
14. Gould. op. cit.
15. Roethlisberger, F.J. and Dickson, W.J., *Management and the Worker*, Harvard University Press, 1949.
16. Herzberg, F.W., *Work and the Nature of Man*, World Publishing Company, 1966.
17. Mayo, E., *The Social Problems of an Industrial Civilization*, Routledge and Kegan Paul, 1949.
18. Argyris, C., *Personality and Organization*, Harper and Row, 1957.
19. Herzberg, F., Mausner, B. and Snyderman, B., *The Motivation to Work*, Wiley, 1959.
20. Likert, R., *New Patterns of Management*, McGraw-Hill, 1961.
21. McGregor, D., *Leadership and Motivation*, MIT Press, 1966.
22. Trist, E. and Murray, H., *The Social Engagement of Social Science. Vol.1, The Socio-psychological Perspective*, University of Pennsylvania Press, 1991.
23. Trist, E. and Murray, H., *The Social Engagement of Social Science. Vol. 2, The Socio-technical Perspective*, University of Pennsylvania Press, 1993.
24. Bertalanffy, L. von, *General System Theory*, Braziller, 1968.
25. Mumford, E. and Weir, M., *Computer Systems in Work Design – The ETHICS Method*, Associated Business Press, 1979.
26. Mumford, E. and Henshall, D., *A Participative Approach to Computer Systems Design*, Associated Business Press, 1979.
27. Mumford, E. and MacDonald, B., *XSEL's Progress*, Wiley, 1989.
28. Hammer, M. and Champy, J., *Reengineering the Corporation*, Nicholas Brealey, 1993.
29. Taylor, F.W., *Scientific Management*, Harper and Row, 1947.
30. Vickers, G., *Making Institutions Work*, Associated Business Programmes, 1973.
31. Handy, C., *The Empty Raincoat*, Hutchinson, 1994.
32. Ibid.
33. Baker, E.F., *Technology and Woman's Work*, Columbia University Press, 1964.
34. Noble, D., *America by Design*, Knopf, 1979.

5 An ethical approach: socio-technical design

Throughout this book there have been frequent references to socio-technical design. Stress has been placed on the advantages of this approach for the systems designer or change agent who wishes to give as much attention to the needs of people as to the demands of technology. In this chapter we will show how socio-technical design has evolved and discuss where it is today.

How it began

Socio-technical systems design was the product of a group of social scientists who came together at the end of the Second World War and formed the Tavistock Institute of Human Relations in London. The Tavistock, or the Tavvy as it is generally known, was established in 1946 by this group, many of whom had collaborated in wartime projects and most of whom had been members of the Tavistock Clinic before the war. The Tavistock Clinic was, and is, a therapeutic establishment led by psychologists concerned with mental health and individual development. This was the initial focus and orientation of the members of the Tavistock Institute, although they were interested in applying their ideas to workers in industry.

During the war members of the group had collaborated on projects, such as the setting up of group selection boards for officers and the establishment of resettlement units for repatriated prisoners of war. They came from varied academic backgrounds – one, Harold Bridger, was a mathematician; another, Tommy Wilson, had qualified as a doctor.

Eric Trist, an important founder member, became aware of the influence of technology on people when he was working in the jute industry in Scotland, in the late 1930s. He was a member of a small interdisciplinary team studying unemployment when the spinning, section of the jute industry was being rationalized. He found that this change in technology caused unemployment, deskilling and alienation. The technical and social systems were acting on each other in a negative way [1].

The new Institute, funded by the Rockerfeller Foundation, was at first a division of the Tavistock Clinic, but it soon became a separate institution. It continued to share the same buildings with the Clinic, which ultimately became a part of the British National Health Service.

Influences on the Tavistock

The early Tavistock Group were greatly influenced by their wartime experiences. Trist had been struck by the efficiency of the German Panzer divisions which linked men and machines together for military purposes. Bridger had been assigned to a special unit, under the direction of Wilfred Bion and John Sutherland, that was developing ideas about 'leaderless groups' and applying these to officer selection and training. Bridger was later to apply these same ideas to the hospital treatment of some of the psychological casualties of the war. He introduced self-motivated 'leaderless' groups to the Northfield Hospital in which he worked, persuading the patients to take responsibility for organizing many of their own activities [2].

Bion had a particularly strong influence on the ideas of the early Tavvy Group. He was a psychologist of the Melanie Klein School who was associated with the Tavistock Clinic and believed in the power of small group therapy. Bion had two major influences on the work of the Tavistock Institute. He convinced them that their role was to work with small groups in industry, helping group members to become aware of those emotional factors that hindered successful performance of the group's task. The Tavistock workers also used Bion's assumptions as a guide to the nature of the work group. This must be of a size to allow close personal relationships, and it must have a capacity for cooperation in achieving its primary task, it must be able to derive satisfaction from the successful accomplishment of this task [3].

The ideas of two other researchers also influenced Tavvy thinking. These were Kurt Lewin in the United States and Ludwig von Bertalanffy in Europe. Lewin had experimented with democratic, autocratic and *laissez-faire* groups in the late 1930s [4]. In 1950, von Bertalanffy published a paper in *Science* on 'the theory of open systems in physics and biology'. This drew the attention of the Tavistock group to systems theory and the notion of open systems [5].

Early projects in coal mining

The Tavistock Institute made its first major contribution to socio-technical theory in 1949 when it began a number of field projects in the British coal industry [6]. Prior to this it had been carrying out action research with small groups in the Glacier Metal Company and this had led to the publication of a book by Elliott Jacques called *The Changing Culture of a Factory* [7]. This described how small group meetings had led to the systematic rethinking and solution of problems and resulted in the setting up of consultative mechanisms at Glacier. But the Glacier project had been directed solely at group relations and social organization. It did not address the question of technology. The coal mining studies were concerned with organizational arrangements that might increase productivity, and technology was clearly an important factor here.

The approach adopted was to consider each production unit as a socio-technical system. The theory underlying this is described in the book, *Organizational Choice*.

The longwall[1] method will be regarded as a technological system expressive of the prevailing outlook of mass-production engineering and as a social structure consisting of occupational roles that have been institutionalized in its use. These interactive technological and sociological patterns will be assumed to exist as forces having psychological effects in the life-space of the faceworker who must either take a role and perform a task in the system they compass or abandon his attempt to work at the coal face. His own contribution to the field of determinants arises from the nature and quality of the attitudes and relationships he develops in performing one of these tasks and taking one of these roles. Together the forces and their effects constitute the psycho-social whole which is the object of study [8].

These studies were carried out in the north east coalfield in Britain. Their starting point was a number of psychiatric investigations carried out earlier by Morris and Halliday who found an epidemic of psychosomatic disorders among miners working under mechanized conditions [9][10]. The early hand-got method of mining had enabled the miners to work in small, tightly knit, self-regulating social groups. Mechanization removed these groups and substituted an impersonal system of mining in which forty or fifty men would be strung out along a coal face, each one responsible for a single task only. The new system required a cycle of work in which different operations were carried out on each shift. If one shift failed to complete its work, men on subsequent shifts would experience serious difficulties. The new system therefore created a situation which bred interpersonal and intergroup conflict.

The Coal Board of the newly nationalized industry was concerned that productivity was not increasing in line with mechanization. Labour turnover and absenteeism were high and labour disputes were frequent. But, despite a request from the Board for a comparative study of a high producing, high morale mine

---

[1] The longwall method was a cyclical method of mining in which a different activity was carried out on each of three shifts. On the first shift the coal was broken up with explosives and shovelled on to moving conveyor belts by a group of miners called colliers or fillers. These worked on faces of perhaps a hundred yards in length and were spread out along the face at distances of several yards from each other. The second shift was manned by conveyor movers whose job was to dismantle the conveyor belts, move them forward to the face which had advanced four foot six inches as a result of the colliers' efforts, and reassemble them. The third shift had two principal activities. One was performed by a skilled man who operated a coal-cutting machine. This cut a narrow slit at the bottom of the new face so that when the coal was shot-fired it had a gap to fall into. The second activity was removing the pit-props from the worked part of the face and letting the roof fall in. This job was performed by a group called packers who, in order to avoid surface subsidence as props were removed, built stone packs to assist a controlled fall of the roof.

and a low producing, low morale mine, the Tavistock team decided to carry out the research without the patronage of the Coal Board and secured a grant from the Medical Research Council. The study asked for by the Board was eventually carried out by a group in the Social Science Department at Liverpool University. This included the author of this book who spent nine months working underground in a colliery called Maypole in the Wigan coalfield [11].

The Tavistock research team was able to make a number of comparative studies in the north-east coalfield. The Durham area offered a wide variety of mining methods, often in the same pit or associated with the same seam of coal, although the degree of mechanization varied considerably from face to face. The research focused on the quality of work roles, the nature of task groups, the prevailing work culture, the climate of inter-group relations and the character of the managing system.

The team began to recognize that if the technical system is optimized at the expense of the human system, the results obtained will be sub-optimal. The goal must therefore be joint optimization of the technical and social systems. These ideas were formulated into a set or socio-technical concepts that were written up in a seminal paper called 'Some social and psychological consequences of the longwall method of coal getting', published by Trist and Bamforth in 1951 [12]. Bamforth had been a coal miner before joining the Tavistock Institute and it was through a visit which he made to his old pit in South Yorkshire that the notion of autonomous groups brought itself to the attention or the researchers. The men there had chosen to work this way, even though their colliery was mechanized, because they were working faces that were short in length. By reverting to the small group form of work organization that had been associated with hand-got methods they secured the advantages of a socially close, co-operative environment while working on a mechanized face [13].

The Tavistock team came to believe that once conflict had been built into a work situation, only structural change could remove it. There was little that could be achieved by means of a human relations approach of trying to change attitudes. But although they believed in trying to optimize both the technical and the social aspects of a work system, their influence on the design of technology was not great. The mining engineers were copying the mass production methods of the factory flow line and following the work fragmentation principles of Frederic Winslow Taylor. The Tavvy researchers were only able to reform the social organization of the work system. Nevertheless, the fact that they were able to do this was a tremendous achievement.

The Ahmedabad experiment

While the mining studies were under way, Ken Rice, a member of the Tavistock Institute, initiated a similar piece of research in the Indian textile industry. This was carried out in the calico mills at Ahmedabad and began in 1953 [14]. Work groups were formed so that interdependent tasks could forge interdependent relationships [15]. This led to increased production and increased earnings for the workers. Rice approached this project as a psychologist believing that individuals, groups and institutions are part of one coherent system. In his view, each can be described by their internal and external environments and by the organization and management of the transactions across the boundaries of what is inside and what outside. He saw the enterprise as a living organism that must be related to its physical and social environment, with organization a means to an end. That end was the performance of the enterprise's primary task while at the same time catering for the emotional needs of those who worked for it [16].

Another Tavistock researcher, Eric Miller, returned to Ahmedabad in the 1970s to see if the autonomous work system still remained after sixteen years. He found that it had mostly disappeared. Changing technology and changing markets had caused the mills to revert to the Tayloristic methods of mass production [17].

Developing theory and practice

Unhappily, this was also the situation in Britain in the late 1950s. The Coal Board, although interested in the Tavvy's ideas, was focused on increasing mechanization and was afraid of disturbing relations with the unions. It did not wish to move to more revolutionary methods or organizing work. At the same time, Britain was moving away from the cooperative wartime concern for production and efficiency to the old adversarial positions on wages and working conditions [18]. The Tavvy needed to find new spheres of influence.

Fortunately these were available. By the early 1960s Scandinavia was showing great interest in industrial democracy and Einar Thorsrud was a prime mover in introducing the ideas and action research methods of the Tavistock group into Norway. Hans Van Beinam in the Netherlands was also active in this field and researchers in different countries were working on similar projects. It was during this period that Eric Trist began to work with the Australian social scientist, Fred Emery. The international network that was to spread the Tavistock message into many countries was in the process of formation.

During the 1950s and 1960s work continued on the theoretical aspects of the socio-technical approach with more and more ideas being drawn from systems theory, particularly the notion of open systems that interact with their environment [19]. Many of the ideas in systems science are derived from biology with its notion of organic wholes. The ideas of the organismic biologists, a school of biology that appeared in the late nineteenth and early twentieth centuries, appealed to the Tavistock researchers. Their psychological and medical backgrounds gave them a sympathy with analogies drawn from the human body. They were greatly influenced by the views of the biologist von Bertalanffy who had generalized organismic thinking into thinking concerned with systems in general [20]. In 1962 Rice was writing:

Any healthy system will resist change, because as a living system its life depends on its ability to establish a steady state at least at the level at which adequate exchange of materials with the environment can take place. It matters little whether the change is initiated inside or comes from outside; it is to be expected that there will be resistance [21].

These biological concepts provided the researchers with a neat, integrated view of the world, but it can be suggested that their appropriateness for describing industrial organizations has never been completely demonstrated.

Nevertheless, considerable theoretical progress was being made, particularly concerning how social and technical factors interact together. The Tavistock research had by now produced

1.   the concept of a socio-technical system,
2.   a view of the organization as an open system,
3.   the principle of organizational choice – the need to match social and technical systems together in the most appropriate way,
4.   a recognition of the importance of autonomous groups,
5.   a better understanding of the problems of work alienation [22].

The Norwegian industrial democracy experiment

The next stage of socio-technical development occurred in 1962 with the start of the Norwegian industrial democracy project. Industrial relations in Norway had avoided the adversarial position adopted by British trades unions and managers and there were good relations and mutual trust between the Norwegian Trades Union Congress and the Norwegian Confederation of Employers. They were therefore able to cooperate in examining a number of industrial problems that would have been considered too delicate to address in other countries [23].

During the winter of 1962-63 the Norwegian Institute for Social Research was invited to undertake research on the problems of 'industrial democracy' and they asked the Tavistock Institute to cooperate with them on the project. A number of researchers were involved, in particular Eric Trist, Fred Emery and Einar Thorsrud. It now became possible to try out experiments in several industries and to develop methods as well as theory.

The first initiative was the 'Participation Project' which began in the autumn of 1962. This was concerned with the notion of 'industrial democracy', as it was interpreted and practised in Norwegian industry. The research had as its principal objective finding an answer to the question 'Under what conditions can more rights and responsibilities be achieved for the individual in the workplace?' The first part of the project concentrated on collecting experiences from other countries as well as from Norway. The Tavistock team also cooperated with Norwegian researchers and institutions that were already working in the field, as well as carrying out their own case studies of worker participation in company decision processes.

The second part of the project was more action-oriented and consisted of experiments, in Norwegian companies, to find out how the work activities associated with production systems could be made more democratic. The team introduced autonomous work groups and other changes in the work situation that enabled the individual worker to exercise more personal control over his or her work environment. All of these experiments were designed to ensure that work organization was closely related to existing technology. The first experiments were in the metal fabrication and pulp and paper industries. Later experiments were in shipping and in services, such as education [24].

Interest in the work spread throughout Europe and also overseas. Swedish and Danish firms introduced their own experiments and there were projects in other parts of Europe, India and North America. For example, General Motors has quality of work projects, incorporating employee involvement as well as job redesign, in 140 of its plants [25]. North American initiatives were reinforced by the existence of an academic literature dating from the 1940s that indicated that participative and humanistic styles of management were more successful than the traditional authoritarian approach. These ideas came from influential academics associated with what has been called the 'human relations' school – Likert, Argyris, Bennis and many others.

In the 1970s and 1980s the ideas of the Tavistock Institute were to be found in the philosophies and legislation of many governments, for example, the German 'humanization of work' programme and the quality of working life legislation of Norway and Sweden. Even Eastern Europe was not immune to this influence: an article in *Sputnik, Digest of the Soviet Press*, in April 1977, describes how economic reform had led to opportunities for 'semi-autonomous teams' in building projects and agriculture [26].

Socio-technical design processes

Socio-technical design follows in the footsteps of Mary Parker Follett by having a clear ethical principle associated with it. This is, to increase the ability of the individual to participate in decision taking and in this way to enable him or her to exercise a degree of control over the immediate work environment. It assists personal participation through organizing work in such a way that decisions on how work shall be carried out are taken by the individual and the work group, rather than by the supervisor. In addition, through recognizing the interaction of technology and social organization and the need to try to optimize the behaviour of both of these, it increases productivity and provides an opportunity for individual learning and the development of multi-skills.

In order to achieve increased participation, productivity and learning, the Tavistock group developed a set of steps and processes for the design of work.

These are described by Emery, Foster, and Woollard in a book, edited by Fred Emery, called *The emergence of a new paradigm of work* [27]. These steps are summarized below.

Step 1. Initial scanning and briefing
Describe the main characteristics of the production system and its environment. Determine where the main problems lie and where the emphasis of the analysis needs to be placed. The description of the existing system should cover – the geographical lay-out of the production system, the existing organizational structure, the main inputs and outputs, the main transformations and variances, the objectives of the system, both production and social. (Note: a variance is a potential problem area – a weak part of the system where deviation from some desired or expected norm or standard can easily occur.)

Step 2. Identification of unit operations
Identify the main phases in the production process which convert materials into products. Each unit operation will be relatively self-contained and will effect some transformation of the raw material.

Step 3. Identification of variances
Identify all variances and note key variances. Key variances are those that significantly affect the ability of the production system to pursue its objectives. A variance is considered key if it affects the quantity or quality of production, or operating or social costs.

Step 4. Analysis of the social system
Identify the main characteristics of the existing social system. This requires the following:
1. a brief review of the organizational structure
2. a table of variance control, noting
   - where the variance occurs
   - where it is observed
   - where it is controlled
   - by whom
   - what tasks are performed to control it
   - what information is needed for control
3. a note of ancillary activities unconnected with the control of variances
4. a description of the relationships between workers (over time or in geographical space)
5. a note on flexibility (the extent to which workers share a knowledge of each other's roles)
6. a description of pay relationships
7. a description of the workers' psychological needs.

Step 5. Worker's perception of their roles
An assessment of the extent to which the workers believe that their roles meet their psychological needs.

Step 6. The maintenance system
An assessment of the extent to which this impacts on, and affects, the production system.

Step 7. The supply and user systems
A description of the way in which these environmental systems impact on the production system.

Step 8. The corporate environment and development plans
An assessment of the extent to which these affect the production system's ability to achieve its objectives.

Step 9. Proposals for change
Finally, all the hypotheses and proposals considered during the process or analysis must be gathered together, considered and turned into an action programme. Proposals for action must contribute to both the production and the social objectives of the system.

In many situations, the Tavistock concept of autonomous work groups was found to be the best solution for achieving both social and production objectives. It increased work motivation and contributed towards participation and power sharing, while at the same time enabling a better control of production problems and easier achievement of production targets.

Socio-technical principles

The use of socio-technical design methods of analysis in many different work situations led the Tavistock group to develop a set of principles for good design. These are described by Albert Cherns in an article in *Human Relations* and are a distillation of the writing and experience of Emery, Trist, Herbst and other members of the Tavistock group [28]. These are as follows:

1. The principle of compatibility
This states that the process of design must be compatible with its objectives. If the objective is to create a participative social system, then this must be created participatively.

2. The principle of minimal critical specification
This principle has both negative and positive parts. The negative part is that 'no more shall be specified than is absolutely essential.' This means that a

considerable amount of discretion is left to a work group. The positive part is that 'what is essential needs to be identified.'

3. The socio-technical criterion
This is that variances must be controlled as close to their point of origin as possible. The fewer the variances that are exported from the place where they arise, the fewer the levels of supervision and control that are required.

4. The multi-function principle
This principle is that people should not be given fractionated tasks. It is more adaptive and less wasteful for each individual or group to have a range of tasks.

5. The principle of boundary location
This principle is that boundary location must be chosen with care and that boundaries require management.

6. The principle of information flow
Information systems should be designed so that information goes directly to the place where the required action is taken. This will normally be the work group,

7. The principle of support congruence
Systems of social support should reinforce required behaviour (e.g. group work should have group payment).

8. The principle of design and human values
The objective of organizational design should be to provide a high quality of working life for the members. The original socio-technical job design principles were:

- the need for a job to be demanding and varied
- the need to be able to learn on the job
- the need for an area of decision taking
- the need for a degree of social support and recognition
- the need to relate work to social life
- the need to feel that the job leads to a desirable future.

9. The principle of incompletion
This principle states that design is an iterative and continuous process.

The socio-technical approach as created by the members of the Tavistock Institute aims to provide a set of precise guidelines for creating democratic organizations that are excellent in both human and production terms. It is based on the concept of organizational choice and on the need to consider the interaction of the social and technical parts of any work system. It suggests how groups can be effectively organized in terms of size, skills, status, roles and tasks and regards responsible autonomy as a crucial element in effectiveness. Because the work of the Tavistock has always been problem-centred, there has been a constant search for new paradigms and methods that would assist the solution of practical problems. This is in contrast to the approach of many social scientists whose work has been focused on the development of theory in isolation from practice.

Evaluation and criticism

No work as successful and pervasive as that of the Tavistock can escape criticism and it is useful to discuss this criticism, test its validity and attempt to understand the reasoning behind it. Criticism can be considered from two aspects – the nature of the criticism and the nature of the group making it, with the one tending to explain the other. Over the years questions have been raised by individuals and groups about both the Tavvy philosophy and approach and their problem solving methods.

Much of the early criticism of the Tavistock approach came from British sociologists. They pointed out that its researchers based their approach on a notion of consensus and common interests and took no account of conflict, disputes or industrial relations problems. They argued that because of this gap, the work of the Tavvy made little contribution to sociological theory and did not provide adequate models for explaining human behaviour [29]. This criticism is valid, but it seems to misinterpret the aims of the Tavistock researchers which were not directed at developing sociological theory. Their psychiatric and medical backgrounds influenced them to adopt a therapeutic role and their mission was to restore sick organizations to health by making work less alienating for the individual. To do this, they needed to understand both themselves and the individual worker and most underwent psychoanalysis to help them to gain this insight.

Two other criticisms came from academics. The first was that their work had a management orientation and was directed at helping to achieve management's goals of higher production and fewer disputes. The second was that the changes which they recommended, and implemented, were superficial and palliative, lulling the workers into accepting the deep rifts and inequities of the present economic system. The first criticism contains an element of truth for the Tavistock team were often, although not always, hired by management. This, however, is the situation of most researchers. But a great deal of their work, for example in the Norwegian industrial democracy experiment, was jointly supported by management and the trades unions. As a group they were not management oriented but sincerely sought to improve the position of workers at every level. The fact that their preferred methods of work organization increased productivity was a bonus, and not an end in itself.

The second criticism has been answered by Richard Brown in a presidential address to the British Sociological Association [30]. He makes the point that, 'Limited and partial improvements now are important to those whose lives are enriched or made easier by them; it is presumptuous to dismiss them because they are less than they might be.'

Other criticisms have come from trade unionists whose objections can be summarized in the following way.

1.   That the studies tend to be limited to the day-to-day work situation and do not include planning, overall control and questions of ownership.
2.   That workers and their trades unions are normally not involved as active participants, but only as the objects of interviewers who are interested in their perception of the changes.
3.   That the technology on the market is taken for granted and socio-technical studies are limited to adapting the local work organization and the workers to a given technology [31].

Trades unions also suggest that autonomous groups require workers to assume managerial responsibilities without receiving managerial pay.

There is some truth in these criticisms, but it has to be recognized that action researchers have to accept the constraints of the situations in which they operate. Also, Arne Sandberg has pointed out how the Tavistock socio-technical studies were a part of the Norwegian experiments in industrial democracy [32]. In his view, these showed that the scope of socio-technical analysis could be widened to include not only organizational choice when the technology is given, but also choice among existing technical solutions [33][34][35]. Socio-technical systems analysis may also be used, and has been used, in projects involving workers and their trades unions and not management, for example, in the Norwegian printing industry [36].

It has to be recognized that, as with any developing research group, the Tavistock philosophy and approach changed over the years. In the early coal mining experiments they assumed roles that were both 'therapeutic' and 'expert'. But, after the Norwegian industrial democracy experiments began, they became firm believers in participation and the involvement of workers in the design of their own work situations.

Criticisms of the Tavistock design methods have been few, for the methodology is clearly a powerful and successful one. One criticism has been that although concerned with technology, and anxious to optimize its use, provided that this did not conflict with the needs of the social system, they did not address directly the question of the design of technology or consider the possibility of technological options. The reason for this may have been that they were not engineers and their views had little credibility with engineers. They were therefore not in a position to influence the design of technology. In recent years a number of engineers have associated themselves with socio-technical design, thus enabling this problem to be addressed. These have included Roberto de Maio in Italy and Howard Rosenbrock in the UK. Today, a great deal of technology is flexible and presents options both in design and use. This helps socio-technical practitioners, but at the same time makes their task more complex, as they now have to consider the design of the work system and the design of technology simultaneously.

Other criticisms are that not all workers want to work in autonomous or semi-autonomous groups; that supervision and lower level management suffers, as many of its controlling and problem-solving activities are transferred to the work groups, and that the real improvement to work, and work interest, is marginal. Again, all of these criticisms contain some truth. Followers of the Tavistock approach do tend to recommend autonomous groups as a structural solution for alienating work; in some projects supervisors have been the losers while their subordinates have experienced considerable gains; in others the enhancement of work interest has not been great. But these are relatively minor difficulties that can often be avoided. In most situations it can be argued that a socio-technical solution, participatively arrived at, will lead to higher job satisfaction and a better functioning work system.

Socio-technical design today

Most of the early Tavistock work was concerned with shop-floor systems and there was a question mark over whether the approach was equally applicable to offices. Later research showed that this was the case [37][38]. There are few problems in using socio-technical principles for the redesign of offices, although there is still a need to learn how to apply the principles to the remote network of employees communicating electronically in the automated office of the future. The Tavistock approach is based on the notion of the small, independent work group, handling a set of tasks with high variety, and managing its own activities.

There is an urgent need for research which will help answer such questions as, 'Can an autonomous group be formed from people who are physically distant from each other, and communicating via terminals?' There is also a need for engineers to design a humanistic technology which makes the machine a servant to man and not a controller of man. One change in technology that can assist man and machines to interact positively and productively is the range and flexibility of the technical systems that are becoming available. In the office, perhaps more than on the shop floor, technical choice is now possible and software can be obtained that is both good for people and good for business. Systems designers with a humanistic philosophy can help users to build pleasant, stimulating work structures around new technology.

The other challenge for the socio-technical approach is to learn how to apply it at the macrosocial level. Can it be applied to the design of large multi-national establishments? Can it apply to senior management as well as to lower level employees?

Conclusions

The history of the Tavistock Institute of Human Relations is a success story. Throughout the years steady, if somewhat slow, progress has been made in spreading its ideas throughout the world. Its enemy has always been the belief that efficiency should be the dominant work value, and that efficiency is best achieved through fractionated work and tight control systems. Today we know better, or should know better. But today's companies need to be persuaded to try a socio-technical approach and the approach itself needs to be rethought and adjusted to the constraints and opportunities provided by new technology and new economic situations

Designing and implementing socio-technical systems is never going to be easy. It requires the enthusiasm and involvement of management, lower level employees and trades unions. It also requires time, training, information, good administration and skill. There must be both leadership and conviction. A belief that humanistic work systems are the right of civilized men and women and a knowledge that the socio-technical approach can offer benefits to all organizational participants, assist the creativity and development of individuals and groups, and help to ensure the continuing commercial success of an enterprise.

References

1. Trist, E., *The Evolution of Socio-technical Systems*, Ontario Quality of Working Life Centre, 1981.
2. Cutcher-Gershenfeld, J., 'QWL: a historical perspective', *The Work Life Review*, 11, 16-24, 1983.
3. Bion, W.R., *Experiences in Groups and Other Papers*, Tavistock, 1961.
4. Lewin, K., *Dynamic Theory of Personality*, McGraw-Hill, ?????.
5. Von Bertalanffy, L., 'The theory of open systems in physics and biology', *Science*, 111, 23-29, 1950.
6. Trist, E.L., Higgins, G., Murray, H., Pollock, A., *Organizational Choice*, Tavistock, 1963.
7. Jacques, E., *The Changing Culture of a Factory*, Tavistock, 1951.
8. Trist *et al.* op. cit. 1963.
9. Morris, J.N., 'Coal miners', *Lancet*, 2, 341.
10. Halliday, J.L., *Psycho-social Medicine: a Study of the Sick* Ssociety, Heinemann, 1949.
11. Scott, W., Mumford, E., Mcgivering, I., Kirkby, J., *Coal and Conflict*, Liverpool University Press, 1963.
12. Trist, E., and Bamforth, K., 'Some social and psychological consequences of the long wall method of coal getting', *Human Relations*, 4, 3-38, 1951.
13. Trist, E., op. cit. 1981.

14. Rice, A. K. *Productivity and Social Organization: the Ahmedabad Experiment*, Tavistock, 1958.
15. De, N., *Alternative Designs of Human Organization*, Sage, 1984.
16. Rice, A. K. op. cit. 1958.
17. Miller, E.J., 'Socio-technical systems in weaving: a follow-up study', *Human Relations*, 28, 349-386, 1975.
18. Cutcher-Gershenfeld, op. cit. 1963.
19. Herbst, P.G., 'A theory of simple behavior systems, 1 and 11', *Human Relations*, 14, 71-94 and 193-240, 1961.
20. Checkland, P., *Systems Thinking, Systems Practice*, Wiley, 1981.
21. Rice, A.K., *The Enterprise and its Environment*, Tavistock, 1963.
22. Hill, P., *Towards a New Philosophy of Management*, Gower, 1971.
23. Emery, F.E. and Trist, E., *Form and Content in Industrial Democracy*, Tavistock, 1969.
24. Ibid.
25. Cutchner-Gershenfeld, op. cit. 1983.
26. Ukrainsky, D., 'To each according to his interests', *Sputnik, Digest of the Soviet Press*, 1977.
27. Emery, F.E. *The Emergence of a New Paradigm of Work*, Centre for Continuing Education, The Australian National University, 1978.
28. Cherns, A., 'The principles of socio-technical design', *Human Relations*, 29, 783-904, 1976.
29. Brown, R., 'Review of research and consultancy in industrial enterprises: a review of the contribution of the Tavistock institute to the development of industrial sociology', *Sociology*, 1, 33-60, 1967.
30. Brown, R., 'Working on work', *Sociology*, 18, 311-325, 1984.
31. Sandberg, A., 'Socio-technical design, trade union strategies and action research', in (eds) Mumford *et al.*, *Research Methods in Information Systems*, North Holland, 1985.
32. Ibid.
33. Herbst, P., *Socio-technical Design: Strategies in Multidisciplinary Research*, Tavistock, 1974.
34. Rosenbrock, H., 'Social and engineering design of an FMS', Paper presented at Cape Conference, Amsterdam, 1982.
35. Mumford, E., *Effective Systems Design and Requirements Analysis*, Macmillan Press, 1995.
36. Odegaard, L., *Tibak til det typografiske fag*, API Publications, Oslo, 1981.
37. Pava, C., *Managing New Office Technology*, Free Press, 1983.
38. Mumford, E. and MacDonald, B., *XSEL's Progress*, Wiley, 1989.

6 Designing for freedom in the ethical company

This chapter examines the concept of freedom and asks if the successful firm of the future needs to offer its employees more of this. It discusses different ways of increasing freedom through better communication and effective consultation. It provides some case studies of how user participation can give employees the opportunity to influence new work structures.

Many philosophers and writers on management in the past have associated job satisfaction and quality of life with freedom. Today's experts are increasingly suggesting that companies too can benefit from employees who are free to make choices, take decisions and use their creativity. In this chapter we will ask, and try to answer, the question: 'How does the ethical company increase the freedom of its employees?'

What is freedom?

Let us try to define this vague concept of 'freedom'. If we wish to have more of it, then we must know what it is we are seeking, and we must recognize that freedom can be defined in different ways. What is freedom to North Americans and Europeans may have no meaning for people who live in other parts of the world. For the poor and oppressed freedom is not being hungry and not being killed. It is freedom 'from' not freedom 'for'.

Ideas on freedom

In America and Europe freedom has always been an important issue and something that liberal groups have striven to increase, but it has had many different meanings. In 1776 the American Declaration of Independence proclaimed the need for political equality and political freedom. In the preamble to the Constitution it declared that the people institute their government in order to:

form a more perfect union, establish justice, insure domestic tranquillity, provide for the common defense, promote the general welfare, and secure the blessings of Liberty to ourselves and to posterity.

In Germany, at the same time, the philosopher Immanuel Kant, saw freedom as conforming to moral law. Only good behaviour was free behaviour. A man was free when his ideal self-determined his behaviour. And the State had an important part to play. If the State imposed laws that regulated society in a beneficial way, then the State was assisting freedom.

In the nineteenth century these ideas were developed by John Stuart Mill in England and by John Dewey in America. Dewey equated democracy with freedom and saw it as the ideal form of social organization – one in which the individual and society blended easily with each other. But Dewey widened the sphere of freedom, believing that democracy must play a role in industry as well as in civil and political life. Like his predecessors, the emphasis was on goodness and harmony. Men and women must think and make choices, but these choices must be for the good of all. In making morally correct choices, the individual grew in knowledge and virtue and gained the respect of others.

In the first half of the twentieth century the views of the Frankfurt School had a degree of influence. The Frankfurt Institute of Social Research moved to the United States during the second world war but was relocated in Frankfurt in 1953. One of its members, Herbert Marcuse, who remained in the United States after the war, saw freedom as threatened by technology and by the values behind its development and use. These views had a considerable influence on student opinion in universities and were often translated into political action. Another member, Jürgen Habermas, was less pessimistic about the future and developed a theory of social interaction and communication which will be discussed later in this chapter [1].

Freedom today means the capacity for choice and its exercise, the absence of constraining conditions and the availability of means. It means equal opportunity for self-development in association with one's fellows, enabling conditions and the encouragement and motivation to take this route [2]. Self-development involves the creation of new capacities and the enrichment of existing ones – in other words a general enhancement in the quality of individual, group and organizational life [3].

The words of Thomas Hobbes may still have relevance today. He wrote:

Liberty, or freedom, signifieth, properly the absence of opposition: by opposition I mean external impediments of motion. With respect to a person liberty 'consisteth of this, that he find no stop, in doing what he has the will, desire or inclination to do.'

We would qualify this by adding that individualism and diversity still require some generally agreed values. For example, an acceptance of the work ethic which requires personal independence to be associated with the desire to do a job well, and a restriction on untrammelled self-indulgence so that the needs of the group are in harmony with the needs of the individual.

Freedom and change

Today's accepted wisdom is that improving efficiency and competitiveness requires making changes. We are told that the business environment is becoming more turbulent, more demanding and more international, so that only the dynamic and evolving company will remain viable. There is no longer any place for the stable, slow-moving firm which relies on the existence of secure, unchanging markets for products which never alter. The argument continues that the successful company will require employees who are intelligent, multi-skilled, able to take decisions and to be creative in their thinking. This concept of freedom means that two sets of interests are now coming together. Employees will welcome more freedom and responsibility, provided that this is not associated with excessive stress, and companies wish to give their employees more freedom as this will increase their ability to compete in the market place.

Firms now require employees who do not fear change, but understand, welcome and can handle it. And they require these employees, as individuals and groups, to be good diagnosticians and physicians in their own areas and jobs, to have the skills and knowledge to change as their situation changes and to be willing to learn and take responsibility. In other words, they need employees who are 'free' to think, to decide and to act. To achieve this, management must create a supportive change culture, a participative philosophy, and an absence of victims. More than anything, they must create and establish a set of shared values, they must willingly accept the viewpoints and interests of others, and they must ensure that there are no unresolved, serious and deep-seated conflicts between groups and individuals. These are objectives which enlightened managers of the twenty-first century should strive towards, even though, like the promised land, they are not easily attainable in the present economic climate.

Learning how to change

How do managers learn to do these very difficult things? John Burgoyne believes that there are three levels of learning in most organizations [4]. First, there is very simple learning. The firm learns how to introduce and manage processes, often production processes. It turns these processes into sets of procedures and keeps them going as a required method of working. Learning at this level assumes that the environment is stable and is not concerned with change. The second level of learning is when an organization can adapt to its environment. It recognizes when markets are changing or have changed, and alters itself to meet these new demands. Often this alteration takes the form of improved performance. The objective behind this adaptation is survival.

The third level of learning is more complex and sophisticated. Managers now try to exert an influence on their environments so that they can exist more comfortably and avoid major crises. They try to improve the performance of their suppliers and to please their customers through better quality goods and service, so that their environment is less turbulent and there is less need for dramatic internal change. This makes them more stable and less concerned with constant reorganization. Controlling the environment in this way requires clear values, a high level of knowledge and the ability to persuade and help others to change their ways. It requires a willingness to agree things collectively, as change should represent the views of all and this, in turn, requires open communication. It also requires an ability to identify the problems in external situations which can be influenced, reduced and possibly removed. And the aim is always to enrich the outside world and not to exploit it. Gregory Bateson tells us that there is also a fourth level of learning. This is learning how to learn [5].

How can a firm start moving towards the mature learning states three and four that the more thoughtful of today's management gurus recommend. Where does it start, what direction does it take, how does it proceed? Perhaps the most critical factor is leadership from the top. Required is leadership which says firmly 'This is the culture of this company. This is how we are all to perform, behave, relate and, most important of all, 'learn' in order to be a *successful* and *caring* company. By 'successful' is meant surviving in a tough and volatile market environment, through providing high quality products and services, and helping those that the firm interacts with to do the same. It also means introducing appropriate, steady and well conceived change and avoiding the traumatic change that comes from major and unplanned-for crises.

This, in turn requires excellent intelligence and communication, so that all employees understand their business environment and the direction in which it is moving at any moment in time. They must understand their own particular skills, competencies and limitations and strive to improve these. It also means running an ethical business with high standards of required and expected behaviour.

By 'caring' is meant providing job satisfaction, a high quality work environment and the opportunity for personal development for all employees at all levels in the company. This is what we mean by 'freedom in work'. It also means caring for customers, suppliers and others who provide the firm with services. It means understanding how they wish to relate to the firm and the kind of support and help that they want it to provide. It also means caring for the immediate environment – the community in which the firm is located – by trying to enhance its quality and refraining from harming it through pollution or damage of any kind. And it also means considering the wider world environment, so that the firm's immediate environment is not protected at the expense of the environments of other countries, such as for example by exporting waste to the third world, or damaging the resources of poorer countries through other forms of exploitation.

All of these things require a leader with strong ethical principles, a broad vision and considerable intelligence at the top of the company. We are looking for a John Harvey Jones or a Pehr Gyllenhammar. We may even find some of these qualities in managers from other countries. The Japanese, for example, have brought to European firms a set of management practices that encourage high standards, efficiency, and an ability to manage change successfully.

Levers for change

Successful action requires four things: the ability to change the way things are done, the ability to achieve objectives, the ability to reorganize and integrate activities once the change has taken place, and the ability to keep the new system operating until it is time for the next change [6]. These four activities have been described as innovation, commitment, organizational efficiency and performance [7]. Change of this kind requires a vision of the future, the ability to inspire others to cooperate by communicating this vision and associating it with desired benefits, the successful creation and implementation of a new system and the ability to manage and sustain this system.

Today, innovation is seen as one of the keys to successful survival. This is more than adaptation or environmental control; it is the creation of new ways of doing things – new products, services, structures, processes, methods and skills. Innovation can take place at all levels in all functions, but it requires people with the freedom to think creatively, who have a capacity for original thought and the ability to turn thought and ideas into something of substance. Just as the values of the top become the values of those lower down in the well integrated company, so creativity at the top will stimulate creativity lower down and creativity, in turn, becomes innovation and an aid to survival.

Successful change, particularly if it is large scale or dramatic, requires shared values and mutual understanding. Commitment to change requires that employees at every level must know, understand and approve the vision of the future that is being striven for. They must appreciate what is involved and how they can personally contribute. Commitment to change is greatly assisted by sincere and accurate communication and free and open discussion. There must be opportunities for those who will be affected to raise issues, ask questions, make choices and participate in the debate on future action. They must also be able to express their ideas, attitudes, feelings, concerns and doubts. In this way barriers to change which arise from limited or distorted communication will be removed and reduced.

Participation, or the involvement of all those who will be affected by change in its planning, design and implementation, has been recommended by many writers for many years [8]. In the United States, Ed Lawler has been advocating an approach called 'high involvement management' as the key to successful change and effective performance in the modern company [9]. High involvement management is the extension of decision-making power, business information, rewards for performance and technical and social skills to the lowest level of the organization. The belief is that the company with highly skilled staff dedicated to its values and interests will gain from the participation of all in decision taking.

Change can be facilitated by appropriate methods and tools which assist the identification and analysis of problems, the effective choice and use of technology and the redesign of work. Rudi Hirschheim and Heinz Klein have suggested that methodologies can reinforce an ethical design orientation by assisting individual and collective self-determination, critical self-reflection and freedom from unnecessary or undesirable social constraints [10]. But, whatever route is taken to successful change, it must be remembered that there is never 'one best way'. There must always be opportunities for choice and debate on what is a desirable and beneficial future and how best to achieve this. In Western organizations the ideal choice situation will increasingly be a group one, although individual interests must be understood and catered for.

What is good communication?

Increased freedom for individuals and organizations requires good communication and relevant information. But what does this mean? Information is an ambivalent and imprecise concept. It is often identified with communication and with meaning, although we do not really understand the relationship between these. And the purpose of communication is not necessarily to provide information. What is communication in one culture may represent noise in another – the delicate verbal formalities associated with preventing a person from losing face which occur in the East can be regarded as time wasting and insincere in the West. Again, communication may be for gossip and to tell jokes, while in conversations that people regard as irrelevant, or where they are afraid, communication can be distorted. It may be directed at keeping an interviewer happy, or preventing a threatening associate from becoming angry.

A number of writers have suggested that if communication could provide clear, unambiguous information in a straightforward way, discussions would become more productive and arguments due to misunderstandings fewer. Discourse would then become rational, positive, and productive. This would lead to greater opportunities for freedom as factors which distort communication, such as values, ideologies, power, psychological compulsions and social constraints, would have less influence.

In a truly democratic discussion, all participants would have an equal opportunity to raise issues by asking questions; all participants would have the right to permit or prohibit certain kinds of discussion; all participants would be able to challenge the truth, correctness, appropriateness and sincerity of what was said, and all participants must be in an equal position to express their attitudes, feelings, concerns and doubts. This kind of communication has been called 'emancipatory discourse' and is seen as an important feature of the neohumanist movement. Neohumanism seeks to change society so that it becomes more emancipated and more equal. It focuses on barriers to this kind of change and sees limited or distorted communication as one of these.

Members of the Frankfurt Institute of Social Research developed these ideas on how society can establish a shared framework of meanings, based on commonly held values, norms and beliefs. Jürgen Habermas called his approach to improved communication, Critical Social Theory. This hypothesized that in a society there were three hierarchical knowledge interests. These were: *emancipation* – in which improved communication increased personal freedom; *mutual understanding* – through better use of knowledge, and *technology* – from which people get their livelihood [11]. Habermas believed that the establishment of improved communication would lead to more stable and efficient societies and organizations. People would work together more effectively if they understood each other more clearly.

Habermas sought to integrate classic German philosophy's stress on freedom with socialism's stress on equality through a theory of 'communicative competence'. He wanted to establish 'ideal speech' situations in which everyone could communicate freely, truthfully and on equal terms [12]. He believed that situations in which there was violence, domination, and other forms of social exploitation caused communication distortions and prevented the development of consensus, co-operation and justice.

Habermas's theory has been criticized as being too idealistic and unattainable. It puts too much emphasis on agreement and insufficient emphasis on the appreciation and recognition of individual differences. Instead of producing more freedom, it could, in fact, restrict the liberty of the non-conforming individual. Nevertheless, Habermas does give us something to aim at. He emphasizes the importance of truthful sincerity. This, in turn, requires that communication is comprehensible and intelligible; that its content is true; that it is legitimate and appropriate in the context where it is used and that it is sincerely spoken [13].

The ideas of Habermas have already had an impact on developments such as the early 'group dynamics' movement and the 'T' groups developed by Kurt Lewin at the Bethel Laboratory. More recently his ideas are to be found in 'sensitivity training', counselling groups and other methods for improving social interaction. At the same time the importance of information is getting more and more recognition. It has been described as the 'soul' of modern life and knowledge as the 'ganglion' of post-industrial society [14]. Technical writers now describe people as information processing machines, and some see us as becoming super-computers able, with the help of technology, to extend our collective knowledge to the whole of society. Others take a more conservative approach and seek to develop methods and tools that enable people to communicate more effectively with each other. The computer has much to offer here [15].

We need to separate the consequences of technology from the processes of designing and introducing it. Both have their part to play in increasing society's freedoms. Information systems can support the human being in work, social interaction and the workings of democracy. They can greatly change organizational life and improve the processes of communication. For example, organizations can suffer from the illegitimate use of authority and power, from tunnel vision, from the restriction of knowledge, and from dysfunctional organizational cultures [16]. Information technology can overcome these by ensuring that knowledge is shared, that norms and values are known, discussed and agreed by everyone affected by them and that creative ideas are encouraged and developed.

Assisting freedom through participation

In the remainder of this chapter we will focus on the design stage of introducing new technology, as this has been the author's principal area of interest for many years. In this context we will define freedom as 'opportunities for choice, this choice assisting the attainment of a desired and beneficial future'. Because we are concerned with behaviour in work situations, the choice situation will be a group one, although individual interests must be understood and catered for.

For choice and decision to reflect the wishes of a group, two conditions are required. The first is 'participation'; the group should contain all interested users of the new system or their representatives. The second is 'effective communication'. All group members must be able to discuss their needs freely and openly, to accept challenge and dissent, and to want to negotiate an acceptable outcome. They must also have the communication skills to speak clearly, unambiguously and with confidence. In effect we are seeking to achieve the 'communicative competence' described by Habermas and, like him, to see freedom as associated with groups, as well as individuals, so that liberal theory encompasses general as well as individual interests. These classical ideas fit with the modern view that successful software development requires the creation of a shared objective and agreement on how this objective can be achieved. This implies that participation, cooperation and effective interaction take place [17].

Over the years the author has been developing a structured approach to the non-technical aspects of systems design with the hope of making it easier for users to become involved in a meaningful way in the design process. It is increasingly being recognized that the involvement of users improves systems design by enabling user needs to be clearly identified and by giving users responsibility for the choice of organizational and technical solutions – the latter being guided by the knowledge of IT professionals. Successful user involvement requires accurate analysis of needs, and effective communication and debate, so that appropriate solutions can be examined and accepted. The ETHICS method described in Appendix A is dedicated to facilitating the achievement of these [18].

Increased freedom through participation –
some case study examples

Let us now consider some examples of participative systems design and assess their contribution to freedom in design and freedom in result.

Asbestos cement

ETHICS came about because of an experience that the author had twenty years ago when assisting a group of computer technologists to design and implement a new system. The systems analysts in an asbestos cement company in Manchester, England, were anxious to change the firm's sales office from a batch to an on-line, terminal-based system for customer accounts. They approached her for help saying that they wanted to associate good organizational and job design with the new technical system. She did a survey of job satisfaction in the sales office and discussed the results of this with all the clerks, bringing them together in small groups. At these meetings a large number of organizational problems emerged and she suggested to the clerks that they should think about how these might be solved.

She then forgot about this request and fed-back the results of the survey to the members of the technical design group. They subsequently designed what they thought was an excellent socio-technical system, called a meeting of all the clerks, described their proposed system and sat back and waited for the applause. To their astonishment there was silence. Then one of the senior clerks stood up and said politely: 'Thank you for you presentation, your ideas are quite good, but while you have been designing a new work structure for our office we have been doing the same thing, and this is how we should like to be organized'. He then produced an excellent blue-print for a work structure that solved most of the office's efficiency and job satisfaction problems.

The systems analysts recognized the quality of the clerks' suggestions and it was the clerks' organizational solution that was used when the on-line system was implemented. By taking control of the design of work procedures surrounding the new system, and being allowed to do this, the clerks secured the freedom to create their own preferred method of working. The author learnt a very important lesson from this experience – one that she has tried to apply ever since. This is never to underestimate a group's abilities. People at any level in a company, if given the opportunity and some help, can successfully play a major role in designing their own work systems.

International bank

The author was next approached by an international bank which wished to use a participative approach when introducing more sophisticated technology into its dealing room [19]. The bank's systems analysts were particularly concerned to involve the dealing room support services who handled paperwork and computer input and were in direct contact with customers. Their keenness to involve staff was due both to the importance of the dealing room to the bank's finances and the undesirability of any adverse staff reaction to the new system, and to their genuine desire to create a better work environment for support staff. Prior to the new system work had been split up into a number of routine jobs, such as form filling and coding, and there was little opportunity for interest and initiative.

The user design group consisted of representatives of the dealers and of the dealing room support staff, together with the senior systems analyst. The dealers wanted new technology to provide them with better and faster information but they did not want their organization of work interfered with. The dealing room staff in contrast were anxious to associate the new technology with major changes in their work environment so that they could get more interest and satisfaction from their work. They decided to remove the existing segmentation of work into narrow, routine jobs and to substitute a team-based system in which each team looked after a currency. This required team members to become multi-skilled so that they could deal with the complicated affairs of customers who bought and sold currency on the money markets, as well as handling routine tasks such as coding and record keeping. This group used the freedom of choice provided by the bank's participative approach to systems design to create an increased level of responsibility and work freedom in their day-to-day activities.

One other example can also illustrate our thesis that freedom in systems design through user participation can lead to choice and the creation of increased work freedom through the redesign of tasks and responsibilities [20].

Rolls-Royce Aerospace

Rolls-Royce Aerospace had a purchase invoice department which dealt with the invoices coming in from companies supplying goods and services to Rolls-Royce. This department had an elderly, low morale workforce with little motivation to work efficiently. It was shunned by young people who refused to work in a place they regarded as a graveyard. Rolls-Royce had decided to computerize the clerical processes in this department in an effort to improve efficiency. And, as the author had lectured the Rolls-Royce systems group on participative design on a number of occasions, the information technology manager decided to try a participative approach with the new system.

A user design group was created with representatives from each section in the department together with the systems analyst responsible for the project. The author acted as facilitator to the group and one of the senior clerks was chosen by the members as their chairman. At the same time senior user management, the Head of Management Services, the Personnel Manager and the full-time trade union official agreed to form a steering committee. Once the design group got to work it became increasingly enthusiastic about the task of analyzing the Purchase Invoice Department's problems and needs. All clerks in the department made a written note of their most pressing work problems and completed the job satisfaction questionnaire. Members of the design group then held small group meetings with their constituents to consider more deeply the reasons for these efficiency and job satisfaction difficulties and to discuss possible solutions. Gradually, the work changes required in the department became clear and were documented as important objectives for the new system. These were discussed with the Steering Committee and approved by them.

The systems analyst accepted the task of creating a technical system that would assist the achievement of these objectives and the design group turned its attention to identifying three alternative organizational structures that would help secure the required improvements. Two of these were based on the socio-technical approach of multi-skilled work teams, each responsible for a relatively self contained aspect of the department's work.

After discussion with the Steering Committee and a meeting with all the clerks in the department, an organizational structure was selected in which teams of clerks would look after all the procedures and personal relations for specific groups of suppliers. Clerks in these teams would aim to become multi-skilled and a time period of two years would be required to achieve this. A number of clerks in the department saw this new structure as too demanding and asked if they could remain on routine work. A service centre was therefore created to handle routine processes such as dealing with the circulation of mail. It was hoped that this would be a temporary structure, with all the clerks eventually wishing to become multi-skilled.

This new structure transformed the department from a low morale group shunned by young employees, to a motivated, knowledgeable group that became of great interest to those departments in Rolls-Royce seeking flexible and knowledgeable staff. Here was yet another example of a group where freedom of decision making and choice had led to more freedom in work, by providing opportunities for responsibility, learning and greater control and autonomy.

These three examples are representative of participative projects carried out at the lower levels of companies. Today, ETHICS is increasingly moving up the hierarchy. It has been used to enable Digital Equipment Corporation salespeople in the US to collaborate with knowledge engineers designing the software for XSEL, one of Digital's first expert systems [21]. It is now being used extensively to assist managers to identify their information needs prior to the introduction of an executive information system. Participating companies include KLM, Dutch Telecom and a number of other Dutch companies.

The author's research has demonstrated that, when given design responsibility, most lower level groups will use this to increase their freedom in work by creating more interesting, responsible and challenging activities which require thought and choice. But higher level groups also like freedom, and participation in design can provide this. Through involvement in the design of XSEL the Digital sales force was able to create the kind of expert system that best fitted its needs. More recently, the managers with whom the author has worked, have been able to mould flexible information systems to their personal needs as well as to the objectives of the larger organization. All groups have welcomed the freedom of choice that being given design responsibility has created.

The systems designer as group facilitator

It is difficult for groups embarking on major organizational change involving new technology to bring this to a successful conclusion without assistance. A person acting as 'group facilitator' can be of considerable help in enabling a design group to achieve its objectives. Ideally, this group will consist of representatives of all users directly affected by the new work system. A facilitator can be an independent person who has no direct interest in the proposed change but is available to help the design group to complete its task. This is the best approach. But, it is not always possible to find such a person and it is not uncommon for the systems designer to find him or herself occupying this role.

The following sections aim to provide some useful information on the processes that a facilitator is likely to have to participate in, and manage, in order to improve the communication and decision-taking competence of the group that he or she is assisting. Also examined are some of the problems and stresses associated with the facilitator's role of assisting change.

Group culture

The first thing to remember is that all groups are different and communication takes different forms in different groups, whether these are in-company, national or international. Helping an Indonesian group to design a new computer system will take a very different form from helping a European or American company. The wise facilitator will get as much advance information as possible on the communication philosophies, practices and likely problems in the part of the world where the client group is located. If it is in the Far East, for example, time will be regarded as extendible, family and group status will be important and rigidly enforced, deference and courtesy will be essential and a loss of face will be regarded as an unforgivable insult.

When firms are located in the same country, there may be major differences in communication culture. Some may be tightly organized, have hierarchical structures and believe that communication must follow and respond to this structure. Others will be flat and flexible and enjoy an open and equal communication pattern. The message for the facilitator is to get as much advance information as possible about the culture and organization of each client group.

Even when firms or departments are apparently organized and run in similar ways, the form communications take may be different, with some based primarily on dislike and conflict and others on friendship and cooperation. The facilitator needs to recognize that he or she is entering an established network of complex relationships. There is a need to be accepted quickly, to clarify the facilitator role and to establish who are the opinion leaders in the client group.

First impressions

The facilitator often has to make an advance visit to the client group to explain the role and to advise on an appropriate group structure for the meetings at which change needs are identified and solutions agreed. At this first encounter it is important to be personable, friendly, confident but unassuming, and be able to describe the project objectives in simple non-technical terms. The advantages of a participative and open communication philosophy and approach must be explained and examples given of how other groups, which have successfully implemented major change, have managed the decision-taking process. It may also be useful to show a video of what happens during a successful design group meeting.

The future users of the new system are now identified and the design group selected. This group should ideally not be larger than ten and should contain representatives of all the groups that will use the system. If there are more than ten of these, then more than one design group may have to be created. It can be helpful to give each member of a new design group a questionnaire and ask them to complete this and return it to the facilitator before the first meeting. The questionnaire gives new members an opportunity to think systematically about the mission, key tasks, critical success factors and major work problems of the work area that they are concerned with and, from this analysis, to identify, and prioritize, organizational design needs.

Group objectives and processes

The facilitator now needs to think carefully about his or her objectives. The design group has to be helped to discuss their work and information needs in a clear, systematic and open manner. If they are designing an information system then they have to be helped to arrive at a group decision on the components of this and, as an aid to good communication, interest, excitement and commitment have to be stimulated and maintained.

This requires a skilful handling of group processes. Communication to and from members of the group must be clear and unambiguous, misunderstandings and problems must be sorted out as they arise, equal participation must be assisted, while at the same time the facilitator must never be seen to dominate or control the discussions. He or she should be a tactful, background figure who quietly encourages the silent to talk and prevents the loquacious from talking too much. At the same time, there needs to be an awareness of time, and of the need for pacing the different stages of the decision making process so that a group decision comes naturally at the end of the allotted period.

Creating a drama

Although the facilitator should try to stay in the background and manage the design group's discussions in a restrained manner, a dramatic event is taking place and this drama should be recognized and encouraged. Ideally, there should be opportunities for *reflection* as well as communication. This occurs when the a group member sits quietly filling in the questionnaire before joining the group for the first session. It is useful if, at the start of the first session, group members are asked to stand up and describe how they see their work mission, key tasks, critical success factors and major problems. This provides an opportunity for *self-expression* and the creation of a role and an identity. Staff are always interested to hear their colleagues describe their jobs and this leads to questions and debate. It is the start of the *group discussion* process.

Other spin-offs

Hopefully, by now the group will have accepted that good communication pays off and can help a group to arrive at a solution that is acceptable to all. The group may also have started to realize that information is something that needs to be shared, rather than protected. This communication process should continue into the future and lead to group discussions on the best way to implement and use the system. A process will have started that may lead eventually to a change in the client's thinking and culture.

Some communication needs

The facilitator needs to assist the design group to do the following:

- Arrive at a common definition of the problem
- Understand needs
- Agree objectives
- Accept disagreement
- Tolerate conflict
- Value reasoned debate
- Accept equality of contribution
- Avoid pressure to conform

All these are assisted if the group has, and is aware of, the important values that they hold in common.

How do effective communication and participation assist freedom for the individual?

The author's experience is that communication and participation do assist freedom. They enable information to be shared, discussion to take place and choices to be made. Those involved, whether systems designers or users, seem to find their use an enjoyable and satisfying experience. When something works well, we need to know why and we shall seek the explanations in this section.

Participation is different from communication. The word means 'to take part'. Communication is less active, among its many meanings are communis – together, and communicare – to share. The terms reinforce each other. Through taking part people are able to share ideas and learn from each other. Therefore, following the ideas of Habermas, in an ideal type of participation which he calls emancipatory discourse the following conditions would apply.

- All participants would have an equal opportunity to raise issues by asking questions.
- All participants would be in an equal position to give and refuse orders, to permit or prohibit.
- All participants would be in an equal position to call into question the truth, correctness, appropriateness or sincerity of what is said.
- All participants would be in an equal position to express their attitudes, feelings, concerns, doubts [22].

In order to take advantage of this ideal situation, if it existed, or even of one that is less ideal, individuals must have verbal skills and be able to communicate effectively. But people, even though they are of the same nationality, do not always understand each other. For example, governments have difficulty communicating with industry, academics have difficulty in communicating with governments, while technologists are renowned for using words that non-technologists do not understand. All of these groups have different visions of the world and because of this they may not trust each other. Successful communication therefore requires more than speaking the same national language [23]. However, a common interest can break down many barriers. Where there is a shared objective, and this usually applies when new systems are being developed, openness and trust can emerge from positive discussion and debate. After this the words spoken need reinforcing with commitment and confirming action. What has been agreed must take concrete form.

Highly effective groups, with members who communicate well with each other, have the following characteristics:

- They are attractive for their members.
- They hold common values and are motivated to abide by them.
- They have a supportive atmosphere.

- Each member is motivated to communicate fully, freely and frankly.
- Each member is anxious to receive communications from others.
- Their is a strong motivation to influence others and be influenced by others.
- There is strong motivation to use the communication process to assist the goals of the group [24].

Successful groups also have a good emotional life. Members encourage, praise, harmonize, observe, gatekeep, record and maintain positive attitudes to each other.

The groups associated with cooperative systems design of this kind are, inevitably, transitional ones. They will not exist for long periods, although their responsibilities may extend from design and implementation to continuous monitoring of the system and planning its development. This was true of the Digital XSEL project. These groups require time to consider what they are doing. Meetings at one or two weekly intervals are better than a project that is compressed into a short time frame and requires intensive work. Good analysis and creativity needs opportunity for reflection, thinking through options, and feeling out what is possible, politically and organizationally [25]. Freedom for a group as opposed to an individual also requires an agreement on values and a willingness to negotiate, even compromise, to secure a mutually desirable end.

Freedom and social learning

The ability to use freedom in a positive manner for the general good requires learning. Members of a design group, both systems experts and users, must understand the needs of the parent organization of which their system will form a part; they must understand the needs of the different interest groups represented in the user design team, and the needs of others who will have to interact with the new system. Most of all, they will need to understand and document their own needs and here simple analytical tools such as ETHICS can play an important role in the learning process. Once common interests are recognized and accepted, and there is a consensus that a problem should and can be addressed, then the group can proceed to gain and utilize knowledge. This knowledge will be objective in that it is readily communicable to all the group members. Knowledge leads to success, and successful outcomes are highly reinforcing. They will stimulate a group to move on to more difficult problems, for the members now have confidence in their ability to succeed.

Freedom and control

Participation, effective communication and increasing knowledge lead to control, and both systems designers and users can shape this control. Social control can be defined as 'the intentional manipulation of relationships or events in order to produce desired outcomes'. Most people like to be in control. It reduces stress, and research has shown that the best performers are those who experience some anxiety, but feel that they are in control of the stressful situation. Being in control means that people can do something about situations which otherwise could be threatening; it gives a sense of ability to cope.

Of course, the design process does not always go smoothly and this is particularly true if a new kind of system such as XSEL is being created. External events may threaten the design process or even terminate it and this can cause serious swings in morale. Now the project manager, or design group facilitator, has an important role in giving encouragement and protection to the group and persuading the company that the project is an important one and should have continued support. There seems to be a strong link between control and stress. Individuals or groups who feel that events are moving outside their control can suffer extreme stress and experience feelings of helplessness. These, in turn, can produce a kind of paralysis in which it becomes impossible to take positive action.

Situations in which people do not want control are those where they feel they do not have the knowledge or ability to handle the situation, or they believe that they can have no influence over the subsequent event. New design groups often have the first of these reactions, saying that they have no knowledge or experience of systems design. ETHICS has a major role to play here, as its analytical tools provide security and confidence. One of the first tasks it requires of the new group is to describe their present work situation. This provides security and confidence, as they are all experts in what they do currently [26].

Freedom, participation and the organization

All the evidence suggests that participation has a positive effect for organizations as well as individuals. It is a necessary condition for effective communication and conversation and this is required at all levels in the organization when major change is being introduced. Nevertheless, it can often produce negative attitudes in technical and managerial groups. Some see requests for participation as a loss of legitimacy in the proposed technical processes. These are perceived as being so advantageous that further discussion is superfluous. Others see too much participation as having a paralysing effect. It will stop things happening or it will impede efficiency. Yet participation, discussion and effective communication are usually an intrinsic part of the viability of major change. The success of new technology depends on the coordinated, disciplined action of various sub-groups including systems designers, R and D teams, accountants, project managers, etc. [27].

In the past the design world has appeared to be more sheltered than the real world. In the design world introducing innovation and managing change has been seen as simpler than it really is. Because technical commitments are made at an early stage, participation can be seen as implying resistance, yet participation is usually a facilitator rather than an obstruction. Today, all groups want open communication and information. They want the opportunity to discuss and criticize, with ideas being judged according to their quality and validity. This need to think, talk and evaluate can conflict with the technologists' brief to get innovation in quickly.

Freedom, participation and the future

There seems to be good evidence that sharing the design task between systems designers and users does increase freedom of choice when new systems are being designed. There is also evidence that most people like participation. They like the sense of being in control, of learning and of interacting successfully and positively with other members of a group. Habermas's notions of 'communication competence' and the 'ideal speech situation' are useful in that they tell us that successful communication requires positive values, common objectives, a tolerance of divergent views, and a feeling that all have an equal right to participate in the debate. But communication is not just a question of words. We interpret what people say and make our response as a result of their facial expressions, the voice intonations they use and their physical movements [28]. Personality and charisma are also important and these are most effectively communicated through face-to-face conversation and meetings [29].

At present, it is those systems designers, facilitators and project managers who support and lead design groups who have the responsibility for helping the group members to achieve these things. In pursuing mutual understanding they elicit, through interaction, a shared understanding of the obstacles to good communication. Progress comes from improved face-to-face contact and conversation and from the learning process that takes place in a social situation. All of these contribute to an 'ideal speech' situation, which assists an agreement on systems objectives and the manner of design and implementation. In this way we achieve better, more acceptable and more liberating systems [30].

Habermas believed that freedom depended on 'removing restrictions on communication' and that communicative competence and an 'ideal speech' situation would lead to a higher development of mankind [31]. Systems designers can contribute to this by striving to increase participation and effective communication in systems design, so that users can choose and create the work and social situations that they like and value. If we do this we shall have taken a major step on the road to freedom and towards the Habermas goals of truth, rightness and compassion achieved by free and rational individuals [32].

References

1. Woodward, K. *The Myths of Information Technology and Post-Industrial Culture*, Routledge and Kegan Paul, 1980.
2. Ross, D. *The Origins of American Social Science*, Cambridge University Press, 1991.
3. Gould, C. *Rethinking Democracy*, Cambridge University Press, 1988.
4. Burgoyne, J., in Pedler, M. and Boydell T. (eds), *Towards the Learning Company: Concepts and Practices*, McGraw-Hill, 1994.
5. Bateson, G., *Steps to an Ecology of Mind*, Paladin, 1973.
6. Parsons, T. and Shils, E., *Towards a General Theory of Action*, Harvard University Press, 1951.
7. Hart, S. and Quinn, R., 'Roles executives play: behavioural complexity and firm performance', *Human Relations*, 46, 543-574, 1993.
8. Mumford, E., *Values, Work and Technology*, Martinus Nijhof, 1983.
9. Lawler, E., *High Involvement Management*, Jossey-Bass, 1986.
10. Hirschheim, R. and Klein, H. 'Realizing Emancipatory Principles in Information Systems Development: the case for ETHICS', *MIS Quarterly*, vol.18, No.1 1994.
11. Habermas, J., *Theorie und Praxis*, Neuwied Luchterhand, 1974.
12. Gouldner, A.W., *The Dialectic of Ideology and Technology*, Macmillan, 1976.
13. Held, D., *Introduction to Critical Theory*, Hutchinson, 1980.
14. Bell, D., *Sociological Journeys*, Heinemann, 1980.
15. Gouldner. op. cit.
16. Hirschheim and Klein. op. cit.
17. Bansler, J. and Havn, E. 'The Nature of Software Work', in V. Besselaar, Clement, A. and Jarvinen, P. (eds), *Information System Work and Organizational Design*, pp. 145-152, North Holland, 1991.
18. Mumford, E., *Effective Systems Design and Requirements Analysis*, Macmillan Press, 1995.
19. Mumford, E., *Values, Technology and Work*, Martinus Nijhoff, 1981.
20. Mumford, E. and Henshall, D., *A Participative Approach to Computer Systems Design*, Associated Business Press, 1979.
21. Mumford, E., and MacDonald, B., *XSEL's Progress: The Continuing Journey of an Expert System*, Wiley, 1989.
22. Hirschheim and Klein, op. cit.
23. Goffman, E., *Forms of Talk*, Blackwell, 1981.
24. Likert, R., *New Patterns of Management*, McGraw-Hill, 1961.
25. Morgan, G., *Images of Organization*, Sage, 1986.
26. Garber, J. and Seligman, M., *Human Helplessness*, Academic Press, 1980.
27. Wynne, B., 'Redefining the Issues of Risk and Public Acceptance: the social viability of technology', *Unpublished*.

28. Carroll, J., *Breakout from the Crystal Palace*, Routledge and Kegan Paul, 1974.
29. Zuboff, S., *In the Age of the Smart Machine*, Heinemann, 1988.
30. Hirschheim and Klein op. cit.
31. Habermas, J., *Communication and the Evolution of Society*, trans. T. McCarthy, Beacon, 1979.
32. Poster, M., *The Mode of Information*, Polity Press, 1990.

7 Designing for the future

This book has addressed the problem of how systems designers can make ethical choices when introducing major change into complex and difficult environments.

The first chapter showed how the past has affected the present by briefly examining the development of industry, technology and systems design over the years. The second and third chapters looked at the employer/employee relationship as a series of contracts, each of which has an ethical component. It was shown how these contracts are deteriorating in human terms and how they might be improved by management adopting a more people-centred approach. Chapter four drew attention to ethical approaches in the past and suggested that the ideas of Mary Parker Follett are relevant for those who wish to improve today's employment relationships.

Chapter five examined the socio-technical approach, developed in the 1940s but still flourishing and more relevant than ever to today's problems. This perceives all organizational change as an opportunity to improve efficiency and the quality of working life by designing for people and their needs as well as for technology.

Chapter six stressed the fact that quality of work life requires freedom and that increasing this in the work situation can be an ethical objective. Chapter seven, this final chapter, attempts to integrate these ideas and to suggest how they can be translated into practice. The argument here is that while an ethical approach to systems design and change can be viewed as morally correct, it also has important other benefits. These include greater efficiency, a more knowledgeable and skilled workforce and, most important, the introduction of major change in an acceptable, stress-free and successful manner. This, in turn, will bring a company economic as well as morale benefits.

This book is written for those systems designers who see their roles as creating systems that are beneficial in human as well as technical terms. The author's hypothesis is that this group is rapidly increasing in number although many are still unsure of the human consequences of the decisions that they take. The purely technical group, which has little or no interest in people, is diminishing in size and is often locked away in research laboratories. Their utopia is a machine one and they have no uncertainties about this. Their route is straight and clear and their promised land a network of computers.

Thirty years ago a scientist with the Rand Corporation called Robert Boguslaw wrote a book called *The New Utopians: A Study of Systems Design and Social Change* [1]. In this he described the new technical groups clustered around computers as 'the utopian social engineers of our times'. He saw these groups as social engineers because they were designing our futures, although this was often without thought or intention. He called them 'utopians' because they were seeking new tools with which to shape their ideal worlds, their perfect society. Unfortunately, this perfect society did not necessarily include people. Boguslaw criticized their visions as 'being concerned with neither souls not stomachs'. He predicted a future in which people problems, when they occurred, would be left for others to handle, while at the same time society would be increasingly, as he put it, 'wagged by its technical tail'.

This book recognizes that society today is still being wagged by its technical tail but suggests that systems designers are now having to confront the social consequences of the world that they are creating. These surround them and will not go away. Many are recognizing that they are social as well as technical engineers. They know that they are good at the technical task. They want to be equally good at the social task and create systems that are beneficial for society as a whole, and beneficial for the groups and individuals located in society. Their utopia is not just well-functioning machines; it is a world in which machines, as well as assisting economic success, also help people to develop their talents, to be happy and to be free.

The new role and philosophy of the systems designer

Probably, the first, and most important choice that has to be made by today's systems designer is that of role. What should his or her functions and responsibilities be? Inevitably this definition of role will be greatly influenced by the demands of employers, but it can also be influenced by the personal values of the systems designer. Unless a job is very tightly contained most of us will be able to influence, to some extent, the nature and shape of the roles that we fill [2]. The challenge will be to create, not a utopia, but a situation which caters for human as well as for business and technical needs. Many of the human consequences of systems design occur, not because of intention, but through default. The systems designer does not foresee how users will be affected by the new system. If this was done many adverse consequences might be avoided.

Our human-centred systems designer will think carefully about the people aspects of systems design, will be concerned with the needs of others and will have a group rather than an individual focus. Relationships will be seen as a series of circles, loops and networks rather than as lines of authority. There will be an awareness of how events and relationships influence each other over time as part of a continuous and dynamic process of innovation and change. Our systems designer will accept mistakes, problems and uncertainties as valuable learning experiences. Whenever possible, these will be brought into the open, discussed and examined without the attribution of blame or penalty. Doing this will reduce the occurrence of errors in the future.

Systems designers, like all good citizens, will mostly agree that their behaviour should be guided by ethical and moral codes and beliefs. The problem is how to do this in work situations where economic factors override all others. Ethical responsibility is always a problem for the individual who has to make choices. These choices are made easier if he or she is a part of a group which holds an agreed set of ethical principles.

In many situations the system designer may have to seek a middle ground where ethical opportunities and constraints are viewed as rational. reasonable and meaningful by those concerned with the new system. The most comfortable role for the ethical systems designer is to advise companies how to do better, and more ethically, the things that they already want to do. Where management is autocratic or uninterested, ethical choice may be arduous, even dangerous. The consequences of an unpopular decision may be loss of job, or even profession.

A viable role for the systems designer in difficult and unsympathetic situations can be what Sanford Lakoff calls 'design mediation' [3]. The systems designer now tries to bring agreements and disagreements into the open where they can be discussed and defended, and decision choices can be made. If possible it is desirable to associate senior management with this process. Hard-liners are often to be found in the ranks of middle management, while top management, once involved, becomes keen to take a more socially responsible position. It also has to be recognized that social problems do not have unique solutions. There may be many different ways in which pragmatism can be combined with ideals.

Zygmunt Bauman, an ethical philosopher, believes that our moral consciousness has been anaesthetized, but not amputated. He says 'It is still there, dormant perhaps, often starved, sometimes shamed into silence, but capable of being awoken' [4]. But being moral has its difficulties. Morality is not a natural trait. It needs to be designed and incorporated into human conduct. Also, human beings are morally ambivalent. No ethical codes can fit human diversity and so moral conduct cannot be guaranteed. Morality itself can be ambivalent. Results always have both good and bad consequences.

An ethical approach requires two things, a person or group capable of moral and intellectual growth and an environment capable of change. We also need an ethic for change which can provide discipline for the process of change and make it possible to let go of old roles and ideas without a loss of identity or confidence [5]. But it must always be remembered that a feature of social change is that while it puts right or reduces the wrongs of yesterday, it also brings with it new wrongs that will have to be corrected tomorrow.

Yet, the well-being of society depends on the moral competence of its members. We want a more human world and it is personal morality that makes ethical negotiation and consensus possible. Personal responsibility leads to morality when it involves a willingness to look after the interests of others. It is moral responsibility, moral intimacy and moral impulses that make a good society possible.

All technical choices require 'social thought'. This is thinking about social consequences and making these an important factor in decisions on what machinery and systems to introduce.

Technology can take either hard or soft paths, with hard being 'control' and soft 'support'. Soft paths will provide job satisfaction and a higher quality of work life, they may even make greater profits. An appropriate choice of technology can have a major, positive impact on the creation of desirable and efficient work systems.

Systems designers must be able to relate individual problems to social issues and to assist the removal of those problems by considering both social and technical alternatives [6]. They also need to be aware of the potential of modern technology to contribute to the solution of social problems. For example, by passing information from one group to another at high speed. But they must be aware that technology has its down-side too. Its effects may be very different from the purposes for which it was introduced. There can be unintended consequences which designers cannot control and may not even be aware of. Knowledge can be increased by careful monitoring of new systems and the identification, examination and documentation of these kinds of problems.

The challenge now is to strive for socially responsible technical choice. This requires a recognition of the importance of social relations when technology is being designed, developed, implemented and used. Technical choice should incorporate the notion of 'designing for a desirable future' [7]. This should include human ambitions and social needs as well as economic success.

Change and strategy

In the eighteenth and nineteenth centuries it was widely believed that thought and reason had an important part to play in social progress. Progress was defined as the creation of a better society in which people were healthier and more comfortable, and no-one went hungry. Change was seen as a passage from one stable state to another with technology a useful instrument for assisting this [8]. Happiness was another feature of the good society and this required freedom. Individuals must be free, there must be free competition and technology must be used to increase economic success. Free people, in turn, would lead productive lives and their characters would be improved by hard work. This, in turn, would create moral dependability, ethical values and individual identity.

In the 1960s and 1970s it was still predicted that society was en route to achieving these benefits and that life by the year two thousand would be a comfortable one [9][10]. We would have a system of production characterized by the dominance of the knowledge workers and the increasing role of theoretical knowledge. There would be an expanding service economy and a predominance of white-collar and professional occupations. Western culture would give increasing priority to self-expression, equality, participation and the general quality of life. Corporations would be transformed into social institutions and managers would be a socially responsible elite with an interest in community affairs and long term growth.

There was no vision of the down-side that we now perceive has accompanied many of these changes. Chronic unemployment that affects white-collar workers and managers as well as the blue-collar group that has traditionally been the victim of change. Harsh conditions for many that remain in industry, with short-term contracts, increased hours of work, greater insecurity and considerable stress. We find these now affecting all levels of the employment hierarchy.

Today, the security of work for many people has been replaced by insecurity and a lack of confidence in the future; stability has changed to fluidity. The things that gave us identity – role, job, function, specialism – have all become uncertain and unreliable. Other kinds of relationship now have to provide the missing security. For example, the gang, the club, the gender group and the age group. But these are not always stable and secure groups. They are liable to disintegration. It is believed that the experience of insecurity is at its most acute whenever social relationships deteriorate [11].

We seem also to be in a situation of what scientists call positive feedback. While negative feedback produces stability as changes in one direction are balanced by changes in the opposite direction, positive feedback produces continual change in one direction only. This can be good for stimulating innovation, but it can also easily get out of control. At present many aspects of our socio-economic situation seem to be in positive feedback. For example, increasing unemployment amongst unskilled young men is leading to rocketing crime figures and the creation of a demoralized and aggressive section of society. Chaos theory tells us that relatively small changes can have major consequences. A recent example is the Baring's trader, Nick Leeson, whose attempt to cover losses bankrupted the bank.

Today's systems designer must also understand the role and importance of power. Power is always a factor in change situations. But there are many different kinds of power. One is *control* with which an individual can cause change directly. There is no need to consult or discuss with other people, it is possible to say 'we or you will do this'. This kind of power is not always purely a management prerogative; powerful shop-floor employees can often exert it over their colleagues. But control, except in emergencies, is not usually a wise use of power. Most systems designers will not have, or wish to use, this degree of autonomy and authority.

A more acceptable degree of power is *influence*. Using this, events and situations can be changed through diplomacy and persuasion. This kind of power also has its dangers, as persuading others does not necessarily mean providing knowledge and understanding.

The lowest level of power is *appreciation*. This is the ability to understand, learn and value what is occurring in the change processes that are taking place, even though these cannot be influenced or controlled. It has been argued that too much time is spent, in both the literature and practice, on how to plan and control and not nearly enough on how to learn [12].

What Ackoff calls 'interactive planning' provides both a learning process and a means for securing beneficial change. This is concerned with designing desirable futures and with the processes that bring these about. Interactive planners are constantly seeking to do things better. They try to improve their performance, and the performance of others, by learning and becoming more knowledgeable and adaptable. Ackoff believes that successful change requires continuous planning and review, so that frequent modifications are made as the system and its environment change. It also requires participation and the involvement of all stakeholders. It requires integration, with all levels providing input from their different perspectives. And it requires co-ordination, so that lateral interdependencies between individuals, groups, functions and activities are recognized, understood and catered for.

Tools for change

This book encourages systems designers to examine their roles, knowledge, attitudes and beliefs so that they can take a more ethical stance when designing and introducing new systems. This ethical stance encompasses all who will use or be affected by a new system, at every level. But the 'significant others' will always be the direct users of the system; those whose work is most directly affected.

To assist systems designers in their search for ethical solutions this book provides a number of analytical tools. In chapters two and three we discussed the different facets of the employment contract, and showed how these had altered in recent years and made suggestions for their improvement. This description of employment relationships as a series of contracts provides a tool for measuring and improving employee job satisfaction. A questionnaire can be designed covering the five contracts and given to both managers and their subordinates. This will provide an analysis of the 'fit' between company and employee needs. Questionnaire data of this kind is always best followed up with small group discussions, so that the reasons for problems can be clearly identified and decisions arrived at on how best to address these. An example of a questionnaire is provided at the end of Appendix B.

In chapter five we examined the socio-technical approach to organizational design and showed how its emphasis on designing for people and their quality of working life, as well as for technology could provide an ethical approach to assist organizational design and business process re-engineering. A major factor in quality of working life is always how jobs, roles and functions are organized. For most people jobs need to have enough variety to make them interesting and challenging, but too much variety will cause pressure and stress. In Appendix

B a detailed example of how to do this kind of design is provided. This covers the identification of needs and problems, particularly information needs, and the redesign of work so as to improve efficiency, effectiveness and job satisfaction.

In chapters two and six great stress has been placed on good communication and consultation as an important ethical vehicle to assist successful change. It is suggested that an ethical approach will always include the involvement of users in the design of systems that they will eventually operate or be affected by. This provides them with the freedom to influence design decisions. Chapter six stresses that an ethical approach has as its aim the increase of freedom for all employees in the company. By freedom is meant an ability to achieve personal as well as company goals. These will include the right to a pleasant, healthy and non-stressful work environment, the opportunity to learn and become more knowledgeable, the right to know about, and participate in, any decisions which will greatly affect an individual's work situation, and the right to the degree of job security that the individual regards as desirable.

The author's ETHICS method which is described in Appendix A provides a tool for enabling users to think systematically about their needs and problems, set objectives for a new system, and develop appropriate technical and organizational solutions that contribute to efficiency and a high quality work environment [13].

Ethical analysis

Few design situations are clear-cut with problems and opportunities affecting everyone equally. Some groups may be winners, others losers, once the new system becomes a reality. More clarity can be given to an often confused situation through asking, and trying to answer, the following questions.

- Is there a real ethical dilemma in this design situation?
- What are the issues involved?
- What individuals or groups are involved (the stakeholders)?
- How does each see the situation?
- What is my own ethical position on the problem?
- Is there a solution that fits with my values and would meet the needs of all the stakeholders (the 'ideal' solution)?
- What would be the benefit of this to each stakeholder?
- Would this solution be acceptable to all groups?
- How could I best negotiate agreement or amendment?
- Are any major difficulties likely to occur in the future if this solution proved acceptable?
- What are the alternative 'next best' strategies if the 'ideal' proves unacceptable?

Stakeholders with whom proposals will have to be discussed will include direct users of the system – those who input or access data. Indirect users are those affected by the system through the way data is used – local management, senior management, IT specialists, trade unions, suppliers and customers.

The following are some common dilemmas that systems designers have to confront.

- Those who input data are a different group from those who access data. The input group receive no advantages from the system, yet have the tedious chore of providing basic data for someone else's benefit.
- Systems that incorporate controls that users find unacceptable and intimidating; the measurement of keyboard strokes, for example.
- Systems where data concerning the performance of a group goes directly to top management who then use sanctions to punish poor performance. The users have no way of monitoring their performance themselves.
- The most difficult dilemma for systems designers is, of course, when their proposed systems are going to displace staff and cause redundancy. There is no easy solution to this problem. Here the system designer needs to work closely with department management and human resource management to ensure that strategies are in place to assist movement to other jobs inside or outside the company.

Two qualities that all ethical systems designers require are pragmatism and trust. Ethical systems design is trying for an ideal, but it also has to recognize the art of the possible. If the philosophy and actions of the systems designer ensure that a new system is 'better' in human terms than it would otherwise have been, a great deal has been achieved. Although large gains should be striven for, small gains should not be regarded as less than satisfactory.

The systems designer also needs to be aware of the importance of 'trust'. Hopefully he or she can trust others, although the complications of company policies often lead to devious behaviour, but it is essential that the user groups that are involved in design can trust their change agent. A systems designer must at all times be frank and open, making clear what can be achieved if interested groups work together on a friendly basis. The interests of one group must not seem to be placed above those of another or, if this is unavoidable, there must be an explanation of why this is the case. Communication and consultation are two of the systems designer's most important tools.

All problems cannot be solved, but at least the systems designer will have the knowledge and reward that a human problem has been understood and something has been done about it. An ethical stance has been taken and moral responsibility has been shown. We end this chapter with a quote from Bauman which stresses the importance of this [14]. He says:

Moral responsibility is the most personal and inalienable of human possessions, and the most precious of human rights. It cannot be taken away, shared, ceded, pawned or deposited for safe keeping, Moral responsibility is unconditional and infinite, and it manifests itself in the constant anguish of not manifesting itself enough. Moral responsibility does not look for reassurance for its right to be or for excuses of its right not to be. It is there.

References

1. Boguslaw, R., *The New Utopians: a study of systems design and social change*, Prentice Hall, 1965.
2. Morgan, G., *Images of Organization*, Sage, 1986.
3. Lakoff, S.A., *Science and Ethical Responsibility*, Addison-Wesley, 1980.
4. Bauman, Z., *Post-modern Ethics*, Blackwell, 1993.
5. Schon, D., *Technology and Change: the New Heraclitus*, Pergamon, 1967.
6. Mumford, E., and Beekman G-J., *Tools for Change and Progress*, CSG Press, 1994.
7. Ackoff, R., *Redesigning the Future*, Wiley, 1974.
8. Schon, D. op. cit.
9. Galbraith, J.K., *The Affluent Society*, Houghton Mifflin, 1958.
10. Veblen, T., *The Writings of Thorstein Veblen*, Vol. 2, Kelly, 1965.
11. Bauman, Z., op. cit.
12. Smith, W.E., 'Power in the design. management and evaluation of organization' in (eds) J-M Choukroun and R.M. Shaw, *Planning for Human Systems*, University of Pennsylvania Press, 1992.
13. Mumford, E. *Effective Systems Design and Requirements Analysis*, Macmillan Press, 1995.
14. Bauman, Z. op. cit.

Introduction to the appendices

This final section of the book has been written as an aid to translating ethical ideas into ethical practice by providing some examples of how to do this. Preceding chapters have attempted to explain and justify an ethical approach for the design and implementation of new computer-based systems. By ethical is meant an approach that takes account of the needs of people at all levels who contribute to the operation of the enterprise, especially those who will use or be affected by new technical systems.

It has been suggested that an ethical approach which focuses on employees, while also taking account of the needs of associated interest groups such as suppliers, customers and other groups in the corporate environment, should ideally have the following objective: every effort should be made to improve the environment in which these groups are located so that they can achieve job satisfaction, a high quality of working life, the degree of security that they seek and good opportunities for personal development.

It has also been argued that these improvements are best achieved by involving employees directly in the system design and implementation processes. Such involvement requires participation in design and implementation decisions, opportunities for group discussion of problems, needs and opportunities and excellent communications in which all interested groups are involved.

Realizing this objective is not easy and this book attempts to assist its achievement by offering a number of simple tools and techniques that can act as development aids for systems designers and users.

Two of these tools and techniques are described in the following appendices. Appendix A describes ETHICS, a method to assist good systems design by incorporating sound diagnosis, multiple objectives and humanistic organizational restructuring into the design process.

The approach is called ETHICS for two reasons. First it is an acronym for Effective Technical and Human Implementation of Computer-based Systems. Second, it is an ethical design approach with the following attributes.

- It involves all interest groups in the design process. This can accomplished at a number of levels. For example, user involvement can be through representatives nominated by the different interest groups, or it can involve all affected staff through E-mail or other forms of comprehensive communication.
- It enables users to exert some influence over their future roles, responsibilities and work environments.
- It provides users with a sense of systems ownership and control. They can influence the use, development and operation of the new system.

These attributes are advantageous to all groups at all levels, irrespective of whether they are clerks, shop floor operatives, specialists or middle or senior management. For example, the front end of ETHICS, called QUICKethics, is increasingly being used by senior management to identify and prioritize their information needs.

Appendix B provides an example of how to give organizational design, or business process re-engineering as it is often now designated, a human face by again involving users in the design processes and enabling them to improve both their efficiency and their quality of working life. This approach can be applied to work processes, functions, departments or specialist groups.

However, there is an important ethical qualification that has to be made with this approach. This is that user design groups cannot be asked, or expected, to make colleagues redundant. If a primary objective of redesign is staff reduction, and this cannot be achieved voluntarily, then participative design cannot be used. The exercise will now be a management one with the possibility of industrial relations problems and loss of morale.

Appendix A The ETHICS method

ETHICS, and its front end QUICKEthics, are described in detail in a previous book in this series – *Effective Systems Design and Requirements Analysis: the ETHICS Approach* (Macmillan Press, 1995). For completeness there follows a quick summary of this method.

The ETHICS method

The ETHICS method consists of a set of logical, sequential and analytical steps that are taken when a new computer-based work system is being designed. Business objectives and job satisfaction needs are taken into account at each stage of the design process, so that the system is designed specifically to meet these objectives and needs at one and the same time. Technology is seen as an important contributor to the achievement of these goals.

ETHICS has three principal objectives. These are:

1. To enable the future users of a new system to play a major role in its design and to assume responsibility for designing the work structure that surrounds the technology. This involves a communication and learning process and a set of simple diagnostic and socio-technical design tools. By socio-technical is meant a design approach which tries to optimize both the use and development of technology and the use and development of human knowledge and skill.
2. To ensure that new systems are acceptable to users because they increase both user efficiency and job satisfaction.
3. To assist users to become increasingly competent in the management of their own organizational change so that this becomes a shared activity with the technical specialists and reduces the demand for scarce technical resources.

ETHICS incorporates the philosophies of participation, effective communication and socio-technical design. It assists user design groups to create a decision *structure* that incorporates all interested groups affected by the new system; a *process*, which enables the design task to be smoothly carried forward from identification of the need to change to successful operation of the new system; and an *agenda*, that allows business efficiency and employee satisfaction objectives to be considered in parallel and be given equal weight. Its acceptance is increasing as it is recognized that human consequences cannot be left to chance or to *ad hoc* adjustments after implementation. The analysis and specification of the social system, the design of jobs and of the organizational unit as a whole, have now become as important as the specification of the technical system.

Through user involvement, effective communication and informed choice the ETHICS method seeks to achieve greater realization of the advantages of new systems. One result of designing systems in this way is to create jobs which are meaningful and fulfilling. At the same time, such systems are likely to achieve a higher level of human efficiency than systems which people feel have been imposed on them, and to which they have little personal commitment.

The ETHICS method includes the following systematic steps:

- Diagnosing user needs and problems, focusing on both short and long term efficiency and job satisfaction.
- Setting efficiency and job satisfaction objectives.
- Developing a number of alternative design strategies and matching them against these objectives.
- Choosing the strategy which best achieves both sets of objectives.
- Choosing hardware and software and designing the system in detail.
- Implementing the new system.
- Evaluating the new system once it is operational.

ETHICS incorporates the following diagnostic and design tools.

1. A framework to assist the identification of mission, key tasks, important constraints and factors critical to effective operation.
2. A variance analysis tool to assist the identification of significant problems and problem areas.
3. A questionnaire to measure job satisfaction.
4. A framework to identify what is likely to change in the internal and external environments.
5. A set of guidelines for individual and group work design.

A user group designing an information system using ETHICS would proceed through the following steps.

Description of mission and key tasks

This will relate to the function, work process, unit or department where the new system will be located.

At the start of the design process the design group will spend some time working out clear answers to the following questions.

1.   Why does the function, work process, unit or department exist? What is it
      trying to achieve?

2.   What important tasks must it undertake in order to achieve its mission?
3.   What are the major constraints which inhibit mission achievement?
4.   What are the critical success factors?

Question one is fundamental as the most important aim of introducing new
technology should be to assist the achievement of the business mission. All
subsequent steps in the design task will be directed at the effective achievement
of this mission.

Diagnosis of needs

The design group next discusses and documents the following:

1. Day-to-day tasks
The day-to-day routine tasks that are associated with the provision of the
business activity in the user area.

2. Efficiency needs
These are ascertained using a technique called variance analysis which has as its
aim the identification of potential problem areas in a system. This knowledge
enables the variance to be avoided altogether or to be more easily and effectively
controlled and corrected if it does occur. (*A variance is defined as a tendency for
a system or subsystem to deviate from some desired or expected norm or
standard.*)
    In ETHICS variances are placed in two categories: *key variances* which are
systemic (built into the system) and occur because of the essential goals and
functions of the user area, and *operational variances*, which stem from the
organizational inadequacies of the old system and the technical and procedural
problems which have inadvertently been built into it. Key variances are often
found at the boundary between one set of integrated activities and another. To
identify variances, a survey is carried out and all potential users of the new
system are asked to describe on paper the key and operational variances that they
experience. Each member of the design group now holds meetings with the users
that they represent to discuss how these problems can be avoided or more easily
dealt with.

3. Effectiveness needs
Here the design group focuses on success factors rather than problems. It asks
the question 'Which critical activities relevant to mission achievement could be
done better?'

Effectiveness is defined as 'doing critical activities better even though these may already be being done well and, if required, introducing new mission-related activities that will further improve effectiveness.'

4. Job satisfaction needs

Job satisfaction is defined in ETHICS as the attainment of a good 'fit' between what employees are seeking from their work – their job needs, expectations and aspirations – and what they are required to do in their work – the organizational job requirements which mould their experience.

**The employee's
job expectations**

Job satisfaction = a good fit between

**Job requirements
as defined by the
organization**

In ETHICS, job satisfaction is measured using a self-completion questionnaire which is given to all employees who will be affected by the new system. This questionnaire is based on the framework below. The wording of individual questions is discussed and decided on by the design group, who may wish to add additional questions of specific relevance to their own particular situation.

The questionnaire covers the following:

Needs associated with personality

Knowledge needs
How, ideally, would each individual or group forming part of the system like their existing skills and knowledge to be used? What opportunities would they like for these to be developed further?

Psychological needs
What are their needs for responsibility, status, esteem, security, advancement and stress reduction, and how do they define these needs?

Needs associated with competence, control and efficiency

Support/control needs
What kind of support services do different users believe will enable them to carry out their work responsibilities more efficiently and with less stress? These

support services will include the information and materials necessary to work at a high level of competence, as well as supervisory support and good working conditions.

What kind of control systems do users believe will assist their motivation, job satisfaction and efficiency? The level and structure of wages and salaries is an important part of any control system.

Task needs

What kind of task structure do different groups of users find motivating, interesting and challenging? For example, to what extent do users want jobs that include elements of the following: opportunities for self management; for developing new methods, services or products; for co-ordinating their own activities and taking organizational decisions; for solving their own problems and monitoring their own progress.

Needs associated with employee values

Ethical needs

How do users at every level want to be treated by management? Do the organization's policies on communication, consultation and participation meet employee expectations? Do other kinds of policy also meet these expectations?

The questionnaire results are analyzed by department, job, grade and age and graphs are printed out for each department or group to be affected by the proposed system, showing on which of the five job satisfaction measures there is a good or bad 'fit'. The results are given to the members of the design group and to all those who completed the questionnaire. The design group members then hold small group discussions with their constituents and explore their job satisfaction problems and needs. These small group discussions have two advantages. First, they provide information on the reasons for problems and bad 'fits'. Second, the act of discussing problems often causes employees to think out possible solutions to these, and this can be a very useful input to the design of the new system. It also gets all potential users involved in the design process.

5. Future needs

The last part of the diagnosis of needs looks at the future. Most technical systems soon become obsolescent in today's rapidly changing environment. The diagnosis of needs must therefore incorporate some forecasts of what is likely to change in the future. This will provide guidance on how flexible the new system needs to be. This part of the diagnosis requires information on likely future change in the business environment.

Objectives setting

The specification of mission and key tasks, the efficiency based analysis of variances, the identification of effectiveness needs (critical success factors), the job satisfaction questionnaire – and the group discussions associated with this, and the diagnosis of future needs will have identified the problems and requirements of different sections, roles and grades. These will all have been discussed, agreed, documented and prioritized.

The next, and most important, step is to set specific efficiency, effectiveness and job satisfaction objectives for the new system. Alternative organizational and technical design strategies are now tested against these and the strategy that best fits the objectives is the one chosen for implementation. This is a key step in ETHICS. The interests of individual members of the design group and their constituents now have to be reconciled with the interests of the design group as a whole and with those of other groups of users. This may require the discussion and resolution of conflicts of interest.

It can be seen that ETHICS closely resembles the Japanese approach to problem solving. Considerable time is spent on a careful, systematic diagnosis of problems and needs before moving to solutions. Users or their representatives are involved in every stage of the diagnosis and objective setting tasks.

Socio-technical systems design
We have stressed previously that ETHICS provides a learning experience for users and systems analysts, particularly those who are members of the design group. So far, they have been acquiring diagnostic skills but they now commence to learn design skills. They also learn about the various technical options that are available to meet their needs and help solve their problems.

The socio-technical approach has already been referred to in this appendix. Its principal objective is to make work more satisfying for the individual and group doing it, while at the same time enabling them to contribute to a high level of technical efficiency. To achieve this it has developed a number of work design principles. These include the following:

1.   *Task integration*
The work system, comprising a number of logically integrated tasks or unit operations, becomes the basic design unit; not the single tasks or operations which form it. The work unit will involve suppliers and customers.

2. *Team work*
The work group becomes the primary social unit, not the individual job holder.

3. *Self-management*
Internal regulation of the system is by the work group itself.

4. *Multi-skilling*
Because the work group is the primary social unit, the jobs of individuals can be multi-skilled.

5. Choice and decision making
Greater emphasis is placed on the discretionary as opposed to the prescribed part of the work roles.

6. Control
People are treated as complementary to machines, not as extensions of, or subservient to, machines.

7. Work interest
Work organization aims to increase, not decrease work variety, but care must be taken not to increase stress.

An ETHICS method facilitator would ensure that a design group understands the socio-technical approach, but there is no compulsion to use it. A design group may decide that other organizational options are preferable. Technical options are also evaluated at this time, and the efficiency and human advantages and disadvantages of each is examined. Finally, the selected technical and organizational solutions are designed out in detail.

The design group's task is not at an end once the new system has been selected and designed. There is now a need for a carefully thought out implementation strategy and, when the system is being implemented, it is essential to monitor closely what is happening. Although the ETHICS diagnostic and design tools can provide useful starting points for systems change, the implementation process requires careful planning and monitoring to ensure that design strategies are staying in line with job satisfaction and efficiency objectives and that objectives set an early stage of the design process continue to be valid. If the change process deviates from the intended course of giving considerable weight to human needs, then mechanisms must be available to bring it back on course.

ETHICS tries to give users design competence through participation and open communication in which all views have validity. Through their informed choice of solution they are in a position to enhance their quality of working life and secure freedom from work that is unpleasant and frustrating.

Use of ETHICS

ETHICS is now used as a tool for the non-technical aspects of systems design – organizational design and quality of work life, as a general problem-solving tool, and its front end, QUICKethics, is being extensively used for requirements analysis prior to the introduction of a management information system.

For more detailed information on ETHICS please see *Effective Systems Design and Requirements Analysis: the ETHICS approach.*

Appendix B   Exercise in socio-technical design

Readers may welcome a more detailed explanation of how to carry out socio-technical design. The following example will give you some appreciation of how to use a socio-technical approach for organizational design or business process re-engineering. The case study is based on the organizational problems of a real company.

The approach described here has been developed to assist the redesign of work systems and processes, so as to bring about increases in business efficiency and effectiveness and in the quality of working life for employees.

Organizational design should reflect the business mission and key objectives of the company, rather than the demands of technology. It can be considered as a three-stage process. First, the process, department or function is rethought and redesigned so that it is better able to meet business needs. Then an appropriate technology is selected that will support this new structure and facilitate the achievement of the business mission. Once installed, the new organizational structure will have to be modified so that the new technology can be used in the most effective way.

If the philosophy of this book and the ETHICS approach are followed, then the redesign task will be managed by a design group consisting of user representatives and the technical systems designers. In the sales office example that follows the design group will consist of representatives from unit management, the sales force, customer administration services and any other groups with a direct interest in the new system, for example, customers.

Ideally, there should also be a steering group, consisting of head office sales management, the manager of the sales office that is being redesigned and, as there are problems with manufacturing, a representative from that function. This group will ensure that any changes proposed by the sales office design group fit with company policy. It may also work at a higher level, considering changes for the sales function as a whole. It is essential that the design group and the steering group communicate with each other on a regular basis throughout the project.

METHODOLOGICAL FRAMEWORK

The methodological framework is based on the socio-technical design principles of the Tavistock Institute, a cybernetic model developed by Professor Stafford Beer, and ideas derived from Business Process Re-engineering and the Quality programmes of W. Edwards Deming. The work of Beer provides a neat analytical model of a 'viable system' and this, in turn, enables clear simple descriptions of work activities to be made.

In the Beer model a firm, department or, our focus here, work process, can be described as a hierarchy of five levels of activity. Each of these levels must be recognized, designed and managed, and must interact smoothly with the others if the work process is to proceed at a high level of performance. The five levels are shown below.

A VIABLE SYSTEM

Level 5	**CONTROL** **Meeting targets and standards**
Level 4	**DEVELOPMENT** **New thinking**
Level 3	**OPTIMIZATION** **Adding value**
Level 2	**ANTI-OSCILLATION** **Preventing and solving problems**
Level 1	**OPERATIONAL** **Day-to-day tasks**

This viable system model assists those responsible for redesign to examine existing work processes at different levels and to set out systematically and comprehensively ideas for an improved system.

The design group will discuss these ideas with all those associated with or affected by the work system. These ideas will be prioritized and a plan of action worked out, discussed, approved and documented.

An important part of the analysis and design will be concerned with information requirements. The Beer Viable System model can also be used for specifying these in the following way:

A VIABLE INFORMATION SYSTEM
(Required information)

Level 5	**Information to monitor performance** **(CONTROL)**

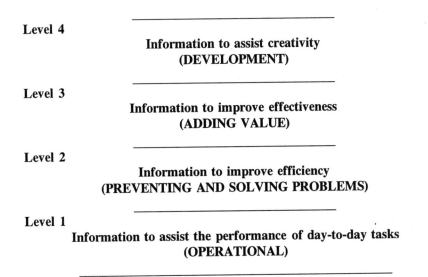

Level 4	
	Information to assist creativity
	(DEVELOPMENT)
Level 3	
	Information to improve effectiveness
	(ADDING VALUE)
Level 2	
	Information to improve efficiency
	(PREVENTING AND SOLVING PROBLEMS)
Level 1	
	Information to assist the performance of day-to-day tasks
	(OPERATIONAL)

The contribution of socio-technical design and the Tavistock Institute is twofold. First, it provides a clear philosophy – that the aim of system design is to optimize both the use of technology and people. Technology should be designed to work as efficiently as possible but, at the same time, the activities of people should be designed so as to provide opportunities for learning and self-development. Second, it also provides a design logic that enables work processes to be analyzed in a systematic, step-by-step manner. These design steps were described in chapter 5. They are set out again below and will be used in this exercise to assist organizational analysis and design.

The Tavistock guidelines

In order to facilitate group performance, the Tavistock team developed a set of guidelines to assist themselves and other consultants or managers who were concerned with improving the design of work situations. The steps below are based on these guidelines.

Diagnosing the problem

Step 1.   Identifying the process

The design group should first specify and clarify the system that is to be considered for reorganization by making a description of its primary tasks and its environment.

The description of the existing system should cover the following: its physical layout, the way work is organized, the main inputs and outputs.

Step 2.   Define the mission, efficiency objectives, critical success factors and major problems (variances)

As any redesign must be directed at enabling a system to achieve its business mission more effectively; this mission must be agreed and clearly stated. Once the mission is written down, major efficiency objectives and critical success factors related to its achievement should be identified. The most serious problems that prevent or slow down its achievement should also be noted.

Step 3.   Describe the environment in which the system is located

This will include internal and external environments. These are systems with which the selected system must interact: the office, departmental or other environments and the external supplier and customer markets.

Step 4.   Describe the process as it is at present (unit operations)

Next, the design group should identify the main stages of the system's business processes. These will be sets of activities which help move the product into its finished state yet which are relatively self-contained. Usually, there will be some kind of discontinuity between each stage – for example, the introduction of a new set of procedures, a new input or an elapse of time.

Step 5.   Identification of variances

The design group should now look in more detail at the system problems or 'variances'. A variance is defined as a weak link in the system where it becomes difficult to achieve required or desired norms or standards. A variance is considered 'key' if it affects the quantity or quality of output, or operating or social costs. Variances should be carefully documented.

Step 6.   Value-adding activities

Activities which add value to the product as it moves through the system should also be noted. This is the 'value chain'.

Step 7.   Work relationships – analysis of the social system

Required work relationships should next be examined and documented. These would cover:

- Who works with whom and how.
- A description of the relationships required between staff for the optimal production of the product.
- A note on the extent of work flexibility. The knowledge that each employee has of the jobs of others.
- A description of earning relationships – the nature of the salary system, differentials, bonuses, etc.

Step 8. Job satisfaction analysis. How staff see their roles

The design group should examine the extent to which staff think that the existing organization of work and their present roles meet the psychological needs of staff. A questionnaire plus small group discussions can assist this analysis. An example of a questionnaire will be found at the end of the exercise on page 151.

Step 9. Development activities

An assessment should be made of how the systems of technical and business support in operation impact on, and affect, the system being investigated. The same should be done for systems that supply materials and services.

Step 10. Strategy and the corporate environment

Information should be obtained on how development plans might affect the future operation of the business system.

Arriving at a solution

Step 11. Proposals for change

Finally, the design group should gather together all this information and, after discussions with the different interest groups associated with the system, should arrive at an action programme. Proposals for action must contribute both to the improvement of the business system and to the improvement of the social system. The latter requires actions directed at improving job satisfaction and the quality of the work environment.

Proposals for change should fit into the Beer framework, as follows:

- **Identify the new mission, efficiency objectives, critical success factors and strategies for overcoming major problems (key variances)**
These must be described first with some care, as subsequent design decisions will be evaluated in terms of their ability to contribute to their achievement.

- **Note the new organization of day-to-day tasks – described as unit operations**

These are the day-to-day or regular activities related to the production of the primary product.

- **Note proposals for controlling potential new and old variance areas**

These are likely to be found at the interfaces between one unit operation and the next.

- **Note proposals for adding value**

Identify those activities that contribute most to the development of the product and establish how they can be carried out most effectively.

Think about introducing new activities, for example, new customer services, which can add value to the work process.

- **New development activities**

When redesigning a system the future must never be forgotten.

Required new developments will come from an examination of the external environment and the changes that are likely to take place there.

- **New business strategies**

Proposals for long-term as well as short term change should be examined and documented.

- **Required relationships**

All these proposed changes will lead to a requirement for new roles and relationships. These must be identified.

- **Required job satisfaction improvements**

The diagnosis of needs will have shown the level of job satisfaction in staff associated with the process. Activities and conditions causing frustration, stress and dissatisfaction must be removed or improved.

- **New measures of performance**

Lastly, wherever targets and goals can be set to measure improvement this should be done. An estimate of improvement often requires a knowledge of the pre-change situation. Whenever possible pre-change measures should be collected before changes take place.

In many situations the Tavistock concept of self-managing groups will be found to be an organizational solution that achieves both business and social objectives, although the degree of self-management permitted will depend on the views of staff and management. A degree of self-management is found to increase motivation and assist the better control of business problems, quality improvement and the achievement of production targets.

Total Quality

Total Quality is a product of the philosophy and ideas of W. Edwards Deming, an American academic who developed many of his ideas at the same time as the Tavistock pioneers. Total Quality focuses on customer requirements and on providing the best possible product and service for the customer. Statistical quality control is used as a means for checking that standards are being achieved. The approach is often perceived as a way of reducing market uncertainty by creating a group of satisfied customers who will stay with the firm because it provides what they want, when they want it.

Deming shared many of the values of the Tavistock group. He believed that a good manager is one who sets up a system, directs the work through subordinates who have a clear vision of their roles and responsibilities, and introduces realistic performance measures which enable staff to monitor themselves. Employees are assisted to achieve these through excellent training and are encouraged to participate in system improvements. Deming, like the Tavistock group, believed in constant improvement, pride of workmanship, breaking down departmental barriers and education and training. He was particularly concerned with the measurement of results.

The Deming philosophy is that any redesign of work must ensure that quality and meeting customer needs is a high priority in organizational change.

The approach described in the exercise accepts the socio-technical philosophy of trying to optimize the contributions of both technology and human skill and knowledge to the production process. To achieve this it incorporates a design philosophy, a decision structure, and a set of clear, agreed objectives.

It must be stressed again that an important part of the socio-technical philosophy is the belief that the future users of a new system should play a major role in its redesign. This requires the creation of design teams, representing all groups using, or affected by, the system. It also requires a steering group composed of senior managers and a facilitator who can help the design teams to complete their task.

In order to show how the approach can be used we need a case study. For this we have chosen a sales office in a major computer company.

Improving Sales Effectiveness
A case study of the Manchester Sales office of
the Classic Computer Company (CCC)

The Company

The Classic Computer Company is an American firm with business activities throughout the world. It is a market leader selling large and small machines and networked systems. Until recently it has performed well and made excellent profits. In the last two years trading difficulties have caused sales to fall and the Company is reviewing and changing many of its strategies and procedures.

Manchester, in England, is a new CCC sales office. It has only been in existence as a separate entity for three years. It is also a large office, with a staff of 68, over half of whom are salespeople. The selling function is split into five groups.

1. The Public and Technical OEM Unit – selling to local authorities and to Other Equipment Manufacturers that use Classic machines in their products.
2. The New Business Unit dealing with first time customers.
3. The Large Account Unit.
4. The Manufacturing and Commercial Unit
5. The Customer Service Unit that handles small accounts.

In addition there is a Customer Administration Service Unit (CAS) which provides administrative support for the Sales groups.

All sales staff see their work mission as assisting the business to grow and to provide a high quality service which leads to a high level of customer satisfaction. The Sales Manager says:

> Our mission is to be successful, to have satisfied customers, to grow and to create a more professional, experienced sales force on the way. That is Manchester's goal.

The Manchester Sales Office covers a wide selling area which includes Merseyside, Cheshire and Lancashire. Its business target is £50 million per annum. Each Sales Unit is responsible for selling the whole range of Classic hardware, software and services in its particular market area and in order to do this it has to have close contact with the District Field Service and the District Software Service. Both of these can provide guidance on CCC policies and also expert help if this is required. Sales executives are also in regular touch with CCC's Head Office Credit Control and Customer Administration Services and with a number of other Head Office Departments; for example, Legal, Marketing and Educational Services.

Roles and responsibilities

A large percentage of each Manchester salesperson's time is spent in the office – an internal study carried out by CCC showed this to be 56%. Office activity is principally associated with attending meetings (14%), talking on the telephone (12%), and preparing quotations and proposals (11%). In contrast only 19% of time is spent in face-to-face contact with customers. One of the objectives of

Manchester management is to increase the time available for customer contact, so that there is more opportunity for selling. This could be achieved by reducing the amount of administration that a salesman or woman has to cope with and by providing more or better human and technical support services.

A great deal of the time that management devotes to administration is concerned with preparing reports and forecasts on people, products and equipment. Salespeople have to spend much of their time dealing with customer requests for information, queries and problems and in reading the constant flow of information provided by CCC on new products and services. Customer requests are for new product information, prices, proposals, technical inform-ation and delivery information. Both sales unit secretaries and the Customer Administration Service (CAS) Unit will answer queries when a salesperson is not available.

Sales Force needs and problems

Salespeople all have needs and problems associated with the coordination, control and problem solving aspects of their jobs.

Unit managers have many internal coordination problems – for example the installation of new computer and work systems into the Manchester Office. The coordination problems of the sales force are associated with groups located outside Manchester such as Central Sales Administration and Manufacturing. Sales Administration systems are seen as 'antiquated, backward, difficult to use and over-complex'. Production dates are never easy to obtain from Manufacturing and delivery dates to customers are not specific but within a period of five days.

Coordinating a variety of activities is an integral part of the sales role. The 'team' or 'team selling' concept is seen as being an important aid to good coordination. Each salesperson is now backed by a resource group which includes software, educational services, field services etc. This group assists good coordination with customers, but has itself to be coordinated. It becomes particularly important in the later stages of the selling cycle. This resource group is located in the Manchester Office's CAS group.

Development tasks are associated with maintaining traditional business and getting new business. Salespeople who handled Other Equipment Manufacturers (OEM's) see themselves as having a responsibility to help their customers identify opportunities and develop into new market areas. Salespeople dealing with small business customers try to think of applications and software which will attract them. This requires a thorough understanding of the customer's business.

Sales behaviour is greatly influenced by the CCC control system of personal goal sheets with 70% of assessment related to meeting financial targets and 30% to quality factors such as customer satisfaction. Success in meeting personal goals will affect a salesperson's salary the following year, although CCC also offers commission on sales. All salespeople are required to produce a monthly report, plus a detailed forecast per customer for the following four quarters. In addition, there are monthly Unit meetings to discuss market sector problems and each Unit Manager has regular meetings with individual salespeople.

The activities that the sales force see as most important, and also most enjoyable, are face-to-face meetings with customers. One describes getting an order as an 'ego trip'. But each two- to three-hour meeting can require three days of administrative work in the office. Although management wishes to reduce this it can have some advantages as the salesperson is available if any of his or her other accounts telephone.

The worst part of customer relationships is having to make excuses when equipment is not delivered on time, or when Manufacturing changes delivery dates and is not able to provide precise information on when a particular machine will be delivered. In the view of the sales group this behaviour is unacceptable.

The principal problems experienced by salespeople vary with their roles. Managers have to deal with a great deal of complexity – coordinating multiple activities, placating customers whose expectations have not been met and 'managing the unusual'. UK pricing policy is seen as inhibiting some selling efforts. Identical products can be obtained more cheaply from the US and many customers know this.

Managers also have the responsibility of personnel management – keeping staff motivated, ensuring that their knowledge is always up-to-date and helping increase their selling ability in line with CCC policy.

The sales force's major problems usually have their source outside the Manchester office. Salespeople complain about the order administration system and the mechanism for pricing products. The CCC price book comes out once a quarter but is followed by messages concerning errata and price changes. This causes particular problems for OEM salespeople who have to pass this information on to the salesmen of their customers. The information is up-to-date but it is not in a form that makes it easy to assemble and transmit to others.

The price book is also always in a state of growth and information is difficult to find. It would be an improvement if prices could be accessed via a terminal and a system to do this is in the process of development.

Deliveries are seen as a major problem both in terms of production and haulage scheduling. Customers are given a six to eight weeks delivery date for a large system and a two to four weeks delivery date for a small system. However, Manufacturing's production times slip and they do this in stages making it difficult for a salesperson to tell a customer when his machine will be ready. The actual delivery of the equipment by the haulage contractor is also uncertain and can take place at any time within a five-day period. In addition, there can be problems of material shortages, incorrect shipments and waiting for parts.

There is also a lack of software advisory support. There is a view that each Unit team should have a software adviser. At present there are not enough software experts to give advice and this means that it is not always easy to find appropriate applications software for a customer.

Salespeople have to spend considerable time building up knowledge of where information of use to them is located, and this is seen as a major problem. Information is held in different places and in different forms. It is often out-of-date, difficult to access and difficult to remember.

Manchester staff

The following are some of the key staff in the Manchester Sales Office.

The Sales Manager – Richard Keen

Richard Keen is 35 years of age. Since joining CCC five years ago he has always worked in Sales. He was made Sales Manager when the Manchester Sales Office was opened in 1990. His personal mission is to make Manchester the number one sales office in the UK. In order to do this he has to sell machines and systems, maintain good relationships with established customers and attract new customers, develop and keep a skilled and effective sales force, create a technically and administratively efficient and up-to-date sales environment and maintain the job satisfaction and motivation of all the Manchester staff. He also has to demonstrate to CCC Head Office that he is doing all these things.

In addition, he has to be able to introduce and manage major change. In his view the role of the Manchester Office will change dramatically in the next five years as new technology appears and the needs of customers change.

His principal anxiety at the moment is that CCC's relationship with its customers is not as good as it should be. He recently commissioned a survey of customer opinion and found that customer needs were already changing. Many customers did not want just to be sold hardware. They wanted CCC to help them to identify present and future business needs and they wanted their CCC salesperson to thoroughly understand their business needs. A customer had told the researcher.

We want a supplier who is flexible price-wise and who will form a partnership with us to develop new systems. We also want a supplier we can influence and who is able to solve our problems. And, most important we want a supplier who keeps his promises and provides honest time tables.

This last comment made by the customer was another of his major headaches. Relationships between Sales and Manufacturing were not good in CCC. Sales continually complained about late deliveries and Manufacturing claimed that this was usually due to mistakes made by salespeople when ordering equipment.

A third intractable problem was keeping his sales force. Other computer manufacturers were continually trying to attract away the best of these, leaving him with the problem of training staff who were new to CCC and did not understand its philosophy and way of doing business, or the technology they were selling.

Unit Manager – Tom Sawyer

Tom Sawyer is 38 years old and he is the manager of the Large Account Sales Unit. He has worked for CCC for ten years and was an engineer before moving into Sales. He sees his role as 'directing the efforts of the sales force'. This involves managing people, identifying and hiring sales talent, identifying management potential, and training and development. His mission is to ensure that his sales force of seven meet the financial and revenue generating goals set by CCC, continue to meet the needs of their existing customers and succeed in getting a number of new large accounts. As his customers are so important to CCC he has to make sure that his salespeople are aware of this and able to inspire confidence and develop long-term relationships. This requires them to acquire a detailed knowledge of the business needs of their customers.

He too experiences problems because of the late deliveries of machines by Manufacturing. He often has to try and explain to an irate customer why this has happened. He can find himself in a situation where he has to apologize for a late delivery but is unable to tell the customer when the machine will arrive. He feels that his team lacks software advisory support. He also believes that he does not always have the information that his unit and customers require. Information is held in different places in CCC and in different forms; it is often out-of-date, difficult to access and difficult to remember.

Also, there are a number of poor systems in the Sales office. For example, there is a sales forecasting system and this should be the Unit manager's most important source of information. It provides a listing of all the projects that salespeople are working on and forecasts what they are likely to sell. But this system is not user friendly, causes a great deal of frustration and can be misleading.

His group can also experience problems with Manchester's Customer Advisory Service (CAS). This has to provide assistance to all the sales units and this can prove too heavy a load for them. Sometimes they have to make a choice of which unit to look after first and this causes annoyance and frustration to the units which are not given priority. He is keen for his salespeople to have less administration and more time to spend with customers and on 'selling'.

He too sees the nature of CCC's business changing and becoming less hardware and more application oriented. He believes he has an important role in assisting CCC to sell business solutions. In his view it is critical that CCC does not move into a low cost, low profit hardware market.

He believes that the job satisfaction of his unit is good and that they see the Manchester sales office as 'forward looking'. However, with the current business problems, he wonders if CCC will be able to offer its staff the same excellent promotion opportunities as it has in the past.

Sales executive – Jean Harding

Jean Harding is new to the CCC sales force. She has been a member of the Small Business Unit for six months. She previously worked in CAS but has always wanted to 'sell'. Her major problem is information and learning where it is located. She is finding that there is no training programme to help her and that she has to learn by hearsay and trial and error. As many specialist advisers are not located in Manchester it is difficult for a new salesperson to know where to contact them. As well as finding some information is in short supply, inaccurate and difficult to access, she is also suffering from information overload. This is caused by the number of sales flashes and sales updates that arrive on her desk. This is often essential information, but she has difficulty in identifying what is relevant – what she must read and what she can skip. She is also finding that she receives a great many requests for information from customers.

All of this means she has to learn quickly if she is to become effective at her principal task of selling small business machines and systems. A major learning hurdle is configuring. All salespeople have to be expert at this and the errors that they make when they are not is a major cause of the relationship difficulties with Manufacturing.

Configuring means identifying and specifying all the different bits and pieces that make up a customer's new system and understanding the relationships between these. Salespeople have to configure for two reasons. First, to give the customer an accurate quotation of what the new system will cost. Second, to write an order for Manufacturing that accurately specifies what the customer requires. Until a few years ago the CCC sales force consisted mainly of ex-engineers who had little difficulty with configuring. In the last few years CCC policy has changed and members of the sales force are more likely to have business, not engineering, experience. This means that learning how to configure can be a major hurdle and it is one that Jean Harding has to surmount.

She feels that her lack of knowledge forces her to take up too much of other people's time and she is embarrassed by this. However, she is anxious to become a useful member of the Manchester team as soon as possible, to sell effectively and to establish excellent relationships with her customers.

Tony Smith – Customer Administration Services Manager

Tony Smith is 30 and has recently moved to the Manchester Sales Office from an administrative job in Head Office. CAS has been created by CCC to provide the sales force with excellent administrative backup. This should release them to devote more time to the critical activity of 'selling'.

Tony has a staff of six and sees his role as assisting the salespeople to provide a high quality service to customers at every stage of order management from the initial contact with a customer to the eventual equipment delivery and request for payment. This involves checking that orders are correct and valid before they are sent to Manufacturing, ensuring that any discount agreements are correct, monitoring order processing and delivery dates, providing a library information service and assisting the salespeople to respond to customer queries and problems.

These activities involve his group in a wide range of activities both within and outside the Manchester office. These cover Field Services, Software, Manufacturing, Credit Control, Central Invoicing, Installations, Distribution and many other departments located at head office. But the groups they are servicing and with whom they have most contact are the salespeople and their customers.

Requests from customers take many forms. Customers may require sales literature or they may have queries about prices or delivery dates. Requests from salespeople are to book orders, to make sure that orders are scheduled, to communicate delivery dates to customers and also any changes to these.

In addition to receiving requests for information, CAS also handles and sends out a considerable amount of information. Sales flashes are passed on to the salespeople, and information from head office on product releases is sent to both the sales force and to customers.

Tony Smith sees his group as doing a good job but as having problems which are increasing in severity. They have a great deal of paperwork to grapple with and although they can monitor many activities, they can not control these. They are also understaffed for the amount of work that they have to undertake and because of their reputation for efficiency, they are likely to get promoted and leave the Manchester office.

Also, because the sales force find them so useful they are constantly being pressured to take on more activities. The salespeople suggest that they should take on more pre-sales activities – for example, checking that agreements are up-to-date and current and have not lapsed and that quotations for discounts are correct. They are also asked if they will accompany the salesperson when he or she visits customers. They will then get to know the customer and his needs at first hand. Another suggestion is that they should hold the sales force's goals on their system and let individuals know how they are performing.

Success is therefore leading to increased pressure and overwork. There is a likelihood that they will begin to disappoint the sales force because they cannot meet all needs in the time available. They are starting to make choices of whose work to do first. Yet when one sales unit is given priority over another, serious relationship problems can begin to occur.

Ronald Roberts – a major customer

Ronald Roberts is the senior IT manager of the Pharmaceuticals Division of ICI in Manchester. He is at present reviewing his Division's IT strategy with a view to extending networks, introducing more personal computers and trying to relate the company's business needs to what IT has to offer.

He is a long term CCC customer but is becoming increasingly unhappy with CCC's service and relationship. He has decided that he wants a supplier who will help him think clearly and creatively about his business strategies and the information implications of these. He wants to be in long term contact with a CCC senior sales executive who understands the pharmaceutical business and can advise him on how its activities and functions can be improved and extended through IT.

As well as improving communication within ICI, Ronald Roberts wants an information system that will link him to his customers and enable him to better meet his customers' needs. He is proposing to greatly extend his network facilities and ensure that these can link into those of ICI's customers.

He is also looking for a high quality of support from the supplier, up to and beyond the time of installation. This will include training, and software and problem solving support. After this he will require good ongoing maintenance.

He is not sure that CCC can do these things. He thinks they need a mindset change. He says:

> CCC must move away from selling boxes and start selling solutions. Most important it must be able to sell company information systems. It has the possibility of a very exciting future. Its machines are good and its networks are good. But today many customers want a supplier who will spend time getting to know their business, see opportunities for them to develop and come over and say 'our product can help you with this development'. CCC is poor at strategic thinking and corporate development. It is a company with many clever people and it is flexible and responsive but it has no concept of organizational development. The problem is getting CCC to answer the question 'Why should we change?'.

The CCC case study has highlighted a number of organizational redesign problems. Here is how you, the reader, in the role of a CCC salesperson might systematically approach these problems, using a step-by-step approach.

Redesigning the CCC Manchester Sales Office

Step 1. Identifying the Process

The first essential task is to identify the process which you wish to redesign. In this instance it is the selling function.

What is the name of this process?

Selling hardware to customers

Describe the process briefly below.

- Interesting a customer in purchasing a machine.
- Negotiating the size, function and price of the system.
- Making a configuration (estimate of parts that the system will require) in order to give the customer a definite price and the Manufacturing plant an accurate order.
- Progressing the order and giving the customer a delivery date
- Ensuring that the customer has appropriate software.
- Arranging training if this is necessary.
- Ensuring that the machine is correctly installed and provides what the customer wants.

Step 2. Define the Mission, Efficiency Objectives, Critical Success Factors and Major Problems (variances).

Now think about, and write down below, the work mission, key efficiency objectives, critical success factors and major problem areas that are associated with this work process.

The work mission is what you are trying to achieve through the process and will certainly include the principal output – the kind of product or service you wish to supply to the customer.

The key efficiency targets are the kinds of standards and measures you wish to achieve at different stages of the process.

The critical success factors are those points in the process which are critical to its successful conclusion in the required time and at the required quality.

The major problems or 'key variances' are those parts of the process where things are likely to go wrong – often because of a shortage of information. A variance is defined as a part of a system which deviates from some desired or expected norm of performance. A key variance is when this causes a major problem and happens for a reason that is hard to control.

Step two is very important, as all design options will be evaluated against their ability to contribute to the achievement of the mission, objectives, success factors and major problems.

The mission of this process is to:

In the short term: Supply a customer with a computer that meets his or her needs at the required quality and within the agreed time period. Ensure that the customer can use the machine effectively and that it will be well maintained.

In the long term: Through providing a good product and service, acquiring an understanding of the customer's business needs, and establishing good relationships and customer loyalty.

The efficiency targets we wish to meet are:

Quality standards and checks to ensure that configuring and costing are accurate, and that the customer receives a machine with no parts missing.

Time standards and checks to ensure that the customer receives the machine at the time it has been promised for.

Knowledge standards and checks to ensure the customer has the knowledge to operate the machine effectively and that the salesperson understands the customer's business needs.

The Critical Success Factors are:

Correct configuring and costing.

Manufacturing producing the machine at the promised time and in working order.

The delivery service delivering the machine at the promised time.

Training and advice being available to the customer once the machine is installed.

The sales person having the time available to gain an understanding of the customer's business and to sell more products.

The major problems (key variances) we experience are:

Configuring errors made by the sales force that cause Manufacturing to do the following:
Return the order to the sales office for correction; produce a machine with parts or cables missing.

Because of these and other problems within Manufacturing customers do not receive their machines at the time promised or the machines do not work.

Configuring errors will also cause the system to be undercosted and the Company may lose money.

Poor customer relationships because of the problems above and because the sales force do not show sufficient knowledge of the customer's business needs.

Step 3. Describe the environment in which the process takes place.

The environment has the following features

The Sales Office is operating in a difficult market environment. Sales are falling and customers are tending to buy from a number of manufacturers. There is no longer brand loyalty.

At the same time Head Office is pressuring the sales force for more and larger sales.

Step 4. Describe the process as it is at present

Now describe in detail how the process is organized and managed at present. It is important to be completely clear about what happens now, before thinking about redesign and improvement.

A simple way of making this description is to divide the process up into a number of unit operations. A unit operation is defined as a set of tasks which are related to each other and which are separated from the next set of tasks by some kind of discontinuity. For example, there is a time gap, or new material or skills are required, or the product moves to a different technology or to a different group or department.

It will help at this stage to make a diagram of the work process. This should show inputs, operations which make a major contribution to product development, and outputs.

First list the unit operations below and then describe each one.

List the Unit Operations in the present process

1. Setting up the sale and agreeing the order
Customer expresses interest in purchasing a machine and receives a visit from a salesperson. Customer requests a specification and a quotation. This requires the salesperson to do a system configuration and provide an estimate of costs. The customer accepts the system specification, price and delivery date. This is turned into an order by the salesperson and is sent to Manufacturing.

2. Progressing the order
Once the order has gone to Manufacturing the customer may require changes to the specification and these have to be communicated to Manufacturing. Manufacturing may start to fall behind the promised delivery date and the customer will have to be informed of this. The customer may require advice on software, how to fit the machine into available space and how to link it with other systems.

3. Installing the machine
Notifying the customer of the definite time of arrival. Ensuring that engineers are available to install the machine. Providing help with its initial running and with training.

There are other activities that must be carried out, although these are not unit operations as they do not take the product a stage forward in the selling process. We will call these 'climate creating' activities. Two of these are:

Maintaining interest
The salesperson continually keeps in touch with the customer's business developments and informs him or her when relevant new products are developed and arrive on the market.

Follow up
Ensuring that the customer continues to be happy and satisfied with the products he or she already has.

Now describe each unit operation in detail including the inputs to, the activities within, and the outputs from the unit operation. Following the 'viable system model', these are:

- the day-to-day tasks,
- the key and operational variances,
- the value chain – where new value is added to the product,
- the intelligence function – information that is sought from outside or comes from outside the unit operation,
- the control structure – measurements or targets that evaluate the success of the unit operation,
- the outputs from the unit operation and where the process is going next.

Lastly, describe the interpersonal relationships that the unit operation requires and any factors relevant to the job satisfaction of the salesperson.

Setting up sale/agreeing order   (Unit operation 1)

Inputs

Interest in purchasing or decision to purchase by customer. Request for a specification and estimate of price.

Day-to-day or regular tasks

Prepare specification for customer. This requires the salesperson to identify the customer's needs and relate these to available hardware and software. It also requires him or her to make a configuration of parts required and specify the relationships between these parts. A cost estimate must also be prepared from the configuration.

Variances

Configuration errors leading to inaccurate costings. When costing mistakes are made the customer may refuse to pay additional money and this may result in expensive law suits. It will certainly cause bad relationships with customers. It is one of the Company's most serious problems.

Value-adding activities

The customer is given a fast, accurate specification and cost estimate which he or she accepts. This saves the salesperson's time and releases him or her for selling to other customers.

Intelligence gathering

Information on the kind of system that will be most acceptable to the customer and on how far the customer can be pushed to buy a larger system.

Control

Measurements of how long the salesperson has to spend with each customer and of the number of configuring and costing errors each salesperson makes.

Outputs

An order to Manufacturing.

Required relationships

With customers and customers' staff. With Manufacturing, especially when configuring errors occur. With hardware and software advisers located in Head Office.

Factors affecting personal job satisfaction

Maintaining good relationships with customers and with Manufacturing. Receiving praise and help from Sales Office Manager.

Progressing the order   (Unit operation 2)
Inputs
An agreement from the customer that he or she will purchase the machine.

Day-to-day or regular tasks
Liaising with the Sales Office Central Administration Service Group who have responsibility for the paper work associated with the sale. Giving the customer advice on software, fitting the machine into available space and any other problems. Dealing with the customer's wish to modify the system. Correcting configuring mistakes that may have been identified by Manufacturing.

Variances
The Central Administration Service (CAS) has to look after all the sales force and cannot give an individual salesperson the assistance he or she requires.
   Configuring errors cause the machine order to travel backwards and forwards between the Sales Office and Manufacturing. This delays the assembly of the machine. It may lead to the promised delivery date not being met.

Value-adding activities
A correct order being received by Manufacturing. The assembly of the machine being started on time.

Intelligence gathering
How the machine is progressing through the assembly process in Manufacturing. New software appearing that may be relevant to the customer.

Control
How the sale fits into the salesperson's required performance goals for the year. Also, how his or her relationship with the customer fits these.

Outputs
A notification to the customer that his or her machine is now ready and will be delivered on a certain date.

Required relationships
Continuing good relationships externally with the customer and with Manufacturing. Good relationships internally with CAS.

Personal job satisfaction
This comes from gaining customer loyalty, successful selling and the achieving of personal goals. Goal achievement will influence the salesperson's salary the following year.

Installing the machine (Unit operation 3)
Inputs
A notification from the delivery company that the machine has been delivered.

Day-to-day tasks
Checking that company engineers have installed the machine and that required software has arrived. Checking that customer training has been organized and that queries and problems raised by the customer can be quickly dealt with.

Variances
The most serious is the machine not working when delivered because a component is missing.

Value-adding activities
The machine being delivered on time and in perfect working order. The customer being delighted with the service that he or she has received.

Intelligence gathering
What the customer is likely to need next, or can be persuaded to buy. Likely changes in the customer's business strategy.

Control
That required performance targets have been met.

Outputs
A report to the Sales Office Manager that the sale has been successfully completed and the customer is happy.

Required relationships
An ongoing good relationship with the customer, Manufacturing and CAS.

Personal job satisfaction
The pleasure of a successfully completed sale and the approval of the Sales Office Manager.

Maintaining customer interest
(Climate creating activity. CCA)

Inputs
Requests from Sales Office Manager and Head Office for excellent performance and demonstration of this.

Day-to-day or regular tasks
Maintaining regular contact with customer. Keeping up to date with his or her business needs. Keeping records of sales, delivery dates, configuring errors, customer complaints.

Variances
Inability to sustain customer's interest or understand customer's problems. Disputes with customers over poor service and problems.

Value-adding activities
Short term: When customer decides to make a purchase.
Long term: Customer develops company and product loyalty.

Intelligence gathering
The sales person will keep up with the latest developments in the customer's industry, business and business strategy. He or she will keep a note of what hardware and software the customer is buying and from whom. He will also keep in touch with competitor behaviour.

Control
Checking that he or she is meeting agreed performance goals.
Discussing the reasons for inability to do this with the Sales Office Manager.

Outputs
The salesperson will continue to communicate with the customer through visits, postal literature, product presentations, etc.

Required relationships
With customer and relevant people in customer's company.
With own company's product development plans.

Personal job satisfaction
Recognition of ability to develop good relationships with customers.

Step 5. Listing variances

Now list below the key and operational variances. Indicate how these might be removed or reduced and rank them in importance from 1-5.

Variance	How to remove/reduce	Rank
Configuring errors	Better configuring accuracy	1
Costing errors	Better configuring accuracy Accurate cost information	1
Machine does not work	Better configuring accuracy	1
Manufacturing does not have machine ready on the date promised	Better liaison with Manufacturing	1
Transport company does deliver when promised	Better management of sub-contractor	2
CAS does not provide good service	Give sales team its own administrative service	3
Inability to understand customer's needs	Better sales force training Salesperson who is industry expert	3

Step 6.   List value-adding activities

Now note where value is added to the product in each unit operation and rank
it in importance.

Value added?	Could more be added?	Rank
When customer signs order	Yes, more attention given	2
When machine arrives on time	Yes, this is a serious problem	1
When machine works as expected	Yes, accurate configuring	1
When customer decides he has had good service	Yes	1
When long term relationship is established	Yes	1

Next answer the question 'Will better information help to remove or reduce
variances and add more value?'

Variance or Value	Nature of information	Rank
Configuring errors	Configuring checker	1
Costing errors	Correct information on prices	1
Manufacturing Progress	Where machine is in the Manufacturing process	2
Carrier delivery date	Precise date when machine will be delivered	3
Customer satisfaction	Problems experienced by customer	1

Step 7. Analysis of the social system

Who works with whom and how

A selling team consists of the Sales Unit Manager, his secretary and the salespeople in the unit. Some unit teams also have an administrator attached to them.

The selling team has to work closely with Customer Administration Services (CAS) although it is only one of CAS's clients.

Selling strategy will be set by the Sales Office manager after discussion with Head Office.

Each selling team will have occasional relationships with Head Office software, financial and other advisers.

Required relationships

The selling team must work as a cooperative unit although the system of individual bonuses means that there may be competition among the members as to who can sell the most.

It must have excellent relationships with CAS as it depends on this group for the efficient administration of an order.

It must also know where advice on customer and other problems is located within CCC and have good relationships with those who provide this.

Work flexibility – knowledge of other roles

Sales people in CCC used to be ex-engineers, but this is no longer the case. Today they are expected to have a knowledge of customer business. This absence of an engineering background means that individual sales people are less knowledgeable about configuring than they used to be and this has increased configuring errors.

The existence of CAS also means that they may have little experience of administration.

CCC sees their primary function as 'selling' and only extends their knowledge in so far as this increases their selling ability.

Salary system

CCC sales people used to be paid a salary without bonus, although the level of this salary would be influenced by sales made the previous year. This system has now been abandoned and a bonus is given for each sale made. Sales have increased as a result of this, but customer relationships have deteriorated.

Step 8.   Job satisfaction analysis

The objective of this is to identify good and bad fits on a number of variables related to job satisfaction at work.

Attempts to remove or reduce bad fits will be made when the work system is redesigned.

A questionnaire that will assist this analysis is to be found at the end of this exercise on pages 151-154.

Job satisfaction good fits

Almost all the salespeople enjoyed their work and were highly motivated.

They particularly enjoyed selling to customers, working with customers on projects and helping customers to solve their business problems.

They also got great satisfaction from finding new customers or new opportunities in the firms of existing customers.

Job satisfaction bad fits

There were two major causes:
The first was annoying a customer because his machine was not delivered when promised.

The second was a machine not working when delivered because a configuring error had led to a missing part. This too led to bad customer relationships.

A less serious problem reducing job satisfaction was the salesperson's inability to get information when he or she required this.

Step 9. Development activities

List below any proposed or likely new developments which are likely to affect a redesigned work system. These will include changes in organizational structures, new recruitment and training policies, new computer-based information systems.

Probable or possible new developments

CCC is considering centralizing some of its activities. Its present decentralized structure is causing too much duplication of specialist activity at a low level.

CCC will shortly be introducing a progamme of employee training to broaden the knowledge and skills of staff and convert them from specialists to generalists.

New computer systems are being developed that will affect sales people. These include an automated quotes system which will provide customers with estimates of costs. And an expert configuring system which could remove the responsibility for configuring from the sales force.

Step 10.   Future strategy

Strategic decisions are likely to be taken in the areas listed below. The nature of these decisions is not yet known.

Possible strategic decisions

In what parts of the world to sell in the future.

Whether to continue focusing on the sale of hardware or move to new products and markets.

Whether to grow or reduce in size.

Now summarize the organizational problems which you have identified.

Summary of organizational problems

Internal problems
CAS
The present organization of the CCC sales office has small sales teams serviced by a large Customer Administration Services Section (CAS).

The rationale for this kind of organization is the desire to free the salesperson from administration so that he or she can concentrate on the selling activity.

CAS does achieve this result, but this form of structure has a number of disadvantages that may offset administrative gains. These are:

1. Many tasks in the sales office are becoming increasingly differentiated and specialized. This makes the office vulnerable if there is sickness or people leave. It also creates small, routine jobs that may decrease job satisfaction and reduce opportunities for personal development.
2. The separation of CAS from the sales teams can lead to sub-optimization and a conflict of interest. The fact that CAS services all the sales teams can present difficulty in deciding on priorities.
3. The present system has different reporting relationships with the CAS group responsible to a Logistics group. These can reduce identity of interest with the selling function.
4. The divorce of sales from administration may mean that CAS becomes less knowledgeable about what is involved in selling.

CONFIGURING KNOWLEDGE
Because of the new policy of recruiting business experts rather than engineers into the sales force, together with a high turnover in sales staff, configuring knowledge is poor. This leads to errors in orders and quotations and subsequent bad relationships with customers.

INFORMATION
Information about new products and prices is essential to the salesperson. This information is often inaccurate, out-of-date and hard to find.

Boundary problems
The three most serious are:

1. Deteriorating relationships with customers because they do not think CCC is providing a good service.
2. Disappointed expectations in customers who want to relate with salespeople who really understand their business needs.
3. Bad relationships between Sales and Manufacturing because of configuring errors and the inability to keep delivery dates.

Redesigning the system

Step 11.   Proposals for change

Proposals for change

After careful consideration of the diagnostic data, and discussions with all staff who will be affected, proposals for change should be formulated. These too will need considerable discussion before finalization and implementation.

Proposals for change will be set out using the viable system model developed by Professor Stafford Beer and described in the introduction to this exercise.

Please read again the mission, efficiency objectives, critical success factors and major problems that you identified in Step 2. Write these in the boxes below, altering them if you think that they need revising to meet future change. Look at step 3 and reassess the market environment.

The mission for the future is to:

> In the short term. Supply a customer with a system (hardware, software, training and other services) that meets his or her needs at the required quality and within the agreed time period.
>
> In the long term. Establish good and continuing business relationships and customer loyalty.

The future efficiency targets we wish to meet are:

> Quality standards and checks to ensure that configuring and costing is accurate, that the system does what is required of it efficiently and without problems and that follow-up service is excellent.

The future Critical Success Factors are:

> Meeting and exceeding customer expectations in the short and long term. Developing trust, confidence and loyalty in the customer.

Major problems (key variances)

> The present ones should have been eliminated or greatly reduced in severity. New ones should not have been introduced.

The future environment

This is likely to become more, rather than less, difficult, with competition for sales increasing and with open systems making customer loyalty more difficult to achieve.

Changes to the organization of work together with improved information systems can make the mission and objectives more attainable. It is suggested that the changes set out below should be discussed as a possible route to improvement.

INTERNAL REORGANIZATION OF DAY-TO-DAY TASKS

It is proposed that the present Customer Administration Service Unit (CAS) shall be removed, although a 'central information' and specialist advice group will remain. This will contain the library, information service and consultants in configuring, software and other specialist subjects.

The new organization will be based on 'selling teams' which do their own administration. Each selling team will take responsibility for, and become expert in, a particular business area; for example, banking and insurance, education, manufacturing, etc. In effect each selling team will operate, and manage itself, like an independent small business.

The advantages of this kind of structure are:

1. With the exception of face-to-face selling, which remains the prerogative of the salesperson, the other tasks can be distributed among members of the selling team. All can be encouraged to become multi-skilled and this will increase the flexibility and knowledge of the group as a whole.
2. It will enable planned development programmes to be designed for each member of the selling team. A new person will gradually increase the number of tasks which he or she can undertake, with the job of salesperson being the eventual goal.
3. This kind of structure provides excitement, challenge and identity of interest. All members of the account team strive to improve the total performance of their team. A team bonus can reinforce motivation to succeed.
4. CCC customers will now have all the members of a selling team to provide information and assistance when this is required. There will be a shared knowledge of the customer's needs and problems.
5. Each selling team now becomes a profit centre; CCC performance awards would now go to the team as a whole, as well as to individual salespersons.

CONFIGURING ERRORS

Each selling team should have a senior salesperson who is a configuring expert and who takes responsibility for organizing the configuring training of the rest of the team.

In addition, the configuring expert located in the central information group will be available to give advice. Eventually, expert systems providing configuring and costing information will be available for access by each selling team.

Orders and quotations will be checked by a designated member of the selling team before customers and Manufacturing receive these.

DELIVERY DATES THAT ARE NOT MET BY MANUFACTURING

This problem cannot be solved by Sales but its impact can be reduced. A member of each selling team should be responsible for developing good relationships with Manufacturing and for keeping track of the progress of a new machine through the Manufacturing assembly processes. If a delivery date cannot be met, a new date should be arranged and this discussed with the customer.

CUSTOMER RELATIONSHIPS

Each selling team should take responsibility for establishing and maintaining good relationships with its own customers. The team should keep up to date with developments in the customer's business and with problems experienced by the customer. It should monitor the use of CCC systems by the customer and act as friend and guide.

ADDING VALUE

Value can be added through paying time and attention to customer needs and interests and ensuring that the customer understands the CCC quality objectives.

REINFORCING THE SOCIAL SYSTEM

The selling team should be both a good working group and a good social group. The team leader should ensure that the personal development of all team members is made a high priority and that the group feel rewarded both materially and psychologically for their efforts. There must be both cooperation and a degree of competition within the team.

The team leader must also ensure that there is good cooperation between all the selling teams. Competition should not lead to dysfunctional rivalry and antagonisms.

WORK FLEXIBILITY

This should be ensured through the multi-skilling policy and individual training programmes. All members of the team should eventually be able to move into a senior salesperson role, if this is what they want.

SALARY SYSTEMS

This kind of team work requires some form of group bonus so that cooperative effort is rewarded. A 'payment for knowledge' scheme also often works well. Salaries are increased as individuals demonstrate that they have acquired relevant new knowledge.

JOB SATISFACTION

It is the team leader's responsibility to ensure that all members of the group have high job satisfaction. Regular meetings should be held, at which problems can be discussed, and there must be a culture of open communication and joint decision taking.

DEVELOPMENT ACTIVITIES

Each selling team must continually review its own needs and objectives and ensure that these are in line with the business policies of CCC. This requires each sales office to be in close and continual touch with CCC senior sales staff and to be aware of any changes in policy.

FUTURE STRATEGY

Each sales office and sales team must also be aware of changes in the market and have strategies available to cope with these.

CONCLUDING COMMENTS

It must be recognized that change is a continuing process. Any reorganization will have only a limited life and must be constantly monitored to ensure that it continues to fit existing business needs. Adjustments must be made as the external environment changes and creates new demands and problems.

JOB SATISFACTION

The use of a questionnaire greatly assists the measurement of job satisfaction problems and needs, before and after organizational changes are made. It also gives a structure to subsequent group discussions on the subject.

Job satisfaction is an important component of the socio-technical approach, as its supporters believe that what people feel about their work is just as important as what they do. If they really enjoy what they are doing then their morale and motivation will be high and they are likely to be efficient and effective as well as satisfied. If, however, their morale is low and they experience feelings of frustration, then they are unlikely to work at high efficiency and they may derive little pleasure from their jobs.

Job satisfaction is defined as a good fit between what a person does and has in his or her job and what he or she ideally wants to do and have. Most people want the following: to use the knowledge which they possess and to increase this; to get a sense of achievement from work; to have access to resources which enable them to work efficiently and effectively; to have an element of personal control so that they can take decisions and make choices, and to have a well designed job that provides the right mix of interest, variety and challenge. This is the framework that lies behind the questions that follow.

JOB SATISFACTION QUESTIONNAIRE

Here is a questionnaire. Please complete it. There are no right and wrong answers. The best answer is your personal opinion. Please place a tick by the answer you agree with.

What is your job?
....
....

How well do you think your skills and knowledge are used in your present job?
Very well used............................
Sometimes well used..............
Poorly used ....

Would you like to have better opportunities to develop your skills and knowledge?
Yes.............
No..............

Is the amount of challenge in your job
Always about right..........................
Only sometimes right........................
Always too little/ too much..................

Would you like to have more challenge in your job?
Yes..............
No...............

What would make your job more challenging?
....
....
....
....

How much responsibility does you present job require?
A great deal........................
Some but not much...................
Very little........................

How much responsibility would you like to have?
More than now..................
About the same................
Less than now.................

How often do you get a sense of achievement from work?
Very often...........................
Sometimes..........................
Hardly ever...........................

What gives you most sense of achievement in work?
....
....
....
....

Does your work provide you with the opportunity to meet people and make friends?
Yes, always........................
Only sometimes...............
No, very little.....................

Would you like more opportunities to do this?
Yes.................
No...............

How often do you find yourself without the information or materials you need to do your job properly?
Hardly ever........................
Sometimes.....................
Frequently........................

How much of your work is checked by someone else?
Very little...........................
Some, but not all.............
A great deal.....................

Would you like to have?
Less checking than now..................
About the same....................................
More checking.......................................

Do you have clear quality and output targets to achieve?
Yes always...
Sometimes, for some things.............
Hardly ever..

Would you like to have more or clearer targets to achieve?
Yes...............
No..............

Is the amount of work you have to do right for the amount of time available?
Almost always...........................
Only sometimes.......................
Hardly ever...............................

Would you like to work under less pressure than you do at present?
Yes...............
No...............

What is the principal cause of pressure?
....
....
....

Does you job allow you to use your own initiative?
Yes, a great deal..................
Sometimes..........................
Hardly ever...........................

Would you like to be able to use more initiative?
Yes...............
No...............

What would you like to be able to do?
....
....
....
....

Does your job provide you with an opportunity to make decisions and use judgement?
Yes, a great deal....................
Only sometimes.......................
Hardly ever..........................

Would you like to take?
More decisions than now................
About the same.................................
Fewer than now................................

How much opportunity do you have to see a piece of work through from start to finish without having to pass it on to someone else?
A great deal...................................
Some opportunity............................
Very little opportunity......................

Would you like to see a piece of work right through more often?
Yes...................
No...................

Taking your job as a whole, do you enjoy your work, or not?
I enjoy it very much.............
I quite enjoy it.......................
I do not enjoy it....................

Can you suggest how your job could be made more satisfying or enjoyable?
....
....

What do you like most about your work?
....
....
....
....
....
....

What do you like least about your work?
....
....
....
....

The results of this questionnaire provide the basis for small group discussions with future users of the system. They are likely to have a good understanding of the causes of problems and some excellent ideas on how job satisfaction can be increased and work frustration removed. Improvements in morale can be assessed by undertaking a second survey, plus group discussions, once the new system is operational.

Rethinking information needs

Once the redesign of the Manchester Sales Office has been agreed, thought needs to be given to rethinking information requirements so that computer support can be improved. Automated configuring and quote systems are in the process of being designed and introduced but the sales force may require an improvement in other sources of information. QUICKethics can now be used to assist the sales people to identify and prioritize their information needs. This diagnosis is done by the salespeople working together in a group, but group meetings are preceded by an interview with each sales person to enable him or her to examine their work roles and carry out a personal analysis of needs before the group comes together. This interview will normally be carried out by the project Facilitator. Here is the interview she conducted with Tom Sawyer, Unit Manager of the Large Account Sales Group.

Facilitator: Tom, it is going to take you a little time to answer the following questions but it will be well worth the effort. It will enable you to think clearly about what you are doing and, most important, write it down. You will have a valuable document which spells out in detail what you are trying to achieve in your job and how better information can help you.

WORK MISSION

'Tom, here is the first question.'

> Step 1: *What are your work mission, key tasks, critical success factors and most serious problems?*

'This is a critical question. It asks you to state what you are striving to achieve in your job. Please fill in the box below.'

Tom's answer was the following:
MY PERSONAL WORK MISSION IS TO:

> To ensure that my sales group of seven:
> a) achieves the financial and revenue goals set by CCC,
> b) continues to meet the short and long term needs of existing customers and
> c) succeeds in getting a number of new, large accounts.
>
> To assist the members of my group to increase their skills and knowledge, stay highly motivated and enjoy their work.

'Tom, now think about what you have written down as your work mission. In order to achieve this mission what are the key tasks you must carry out? Write these in the box below.'

Tom wrote:
MY PRINCIPAL KEY TASKS ARE:

- Meeting the sales targets that CCC have set for my group.
- Helping my group to establish and maintain good relationships with customers.
- Solving problems for customers and members of my group.
- Developing and implementing a selling strategy.
- Ensuring that my group have the necessary training, information and resources they require.

'Tom, now decide what are the critical success factors which tell you when you have successfully achieved your key task. Write these below.' Tom wrote:

MY CRITICAL SUCCESS FACTORS ARE:

- Meeting or beating CCC selling targets.
- Maintaining loyalty to CCC in established customers.
- Maintaining good customer relations. This requires:
keeping promised delivery dates,
delivering machines that are in 100% working order.
- Maintaining staff high morale and motivation.

'And what are your most serious problems?'

MY MOST SERIOUS PROBLEMS ARE:

- Problems with customers because of late delivery of machines.
- Problems because of a lack of software advisory support.
- Problems because of a lack of information.
- Problems with CCC through losing customers or not attracting new ones.

'Now Tom, will you read through these again and write down below the information you require if you are to achieve your mission, attain your critical success factors and avoid or minimize your difficult problems. We will call this your **WORK ROLE INFORMATION**.'

Key tasks will be looked at in turn once the WORK ROLE information is documented.

THE WORK ROLE INFORMATION I REQUIRE IS:

- **To achieve my work mission**
1. Information on all the projects my sales group is working on and forecasts of what they are likely to sell.
2. Information on the skills and knowledge of each salesperson, the courses that they have taken and those they need to take.

- **To complete my key tasks**
3. Knowledge of sales targets and progress in meeting these.
4. Knowledge of state of customer relationships.
5. Knowledge of resources available to group.

- **To attain my critical success factors**
1. above.
3. Information on how my Unit's customers are reacting to the service they are getting.
4. Information on whether delivery dates are being kept.
5. Information on the number of configuring errors that are being made by my group.

- **To avoid or reduce problems**
  All the information above.

'Now let's look at your responsibilities and your information needs in more detail, Tom. Let's start with your most important key task.'

Step 2: *Describe your most important key task*

MY MOST IMPORTANT KEY TASK IS:

Achieving the sales targets that my group has agreed to meet or beat during the year.

'What are the principal objectives that this task has to achieve?'

THE OBJECTIVES OF THIS KEY TASK ARE:

- To keep the loyalty of existing customers.
- To attract new large account customers.
- To create and maintain customer satisfaction.
- To create and maintain staff motivation and job satisfaction.

'Will you describe the critical factors which determine the success of this particular key task and the major problems which hinder success?'

Tom said that these were the following:

MY CRITICAL SUCCESS FACTORS FOR THIS KEY TASK ARE:

- Establishing and maintaining good relationships with new and established customers. This requires:
  Providing a good ongoing service for all customers.
  Having and showing a good knowledge of the customer's business and information needs.
- Finding new customers in a highly competitive market

'And what are your major problems?'

MY MAJOR PROBLEMS ARE:

- Avoiding customer problems such as late deliveries.
- Salespeople leaving and being hard to replace.

'What are the day-to-day or regular activities involved in doing this task?'

MY DAY-TO-DAY ACTIVITIES INVOLVE:

- Ensuring that my group of salespeople are deployed in the most effective way.
- Dealing with important new customers myself.
- Handling difficult customer queries and problems.
- Ensuring that records are kept of all customers handled by the Unit.
- Ensuring that my salespeople get necessary training.
- Giving them the assistance and encouragement they need.

'Tom, what are the likely problems that must be avoided or corrected?'

PROBLEM AREAS INVOLVE:

- Problems with customers arising from late deliveries.
- Problems with Manufacturing due to incorrect orders.
- Problems with Customer Administrative Services (CAS) because they are not giving the Unit the amount of attention we require.
- Problems due to poor information on price changes, new models etc.

'Which of you day-to-day and problem solving activities require coordination with other departments, managers or groups?'

Activity:	Requires coordination with:
• the administration of orders	Customer Administration Services
• choosing software for customers	Head Office customer advisory service
• giving customers delivery dates	Manufacturing
• Information on invoices, payments, services	Head Office departments

'What targets do you or others set for this task and how is their achievement monitored?'

MY CONTROL ACTIVITIES INVOLVE: **Achievement is monitored by:**

• Targets for the unit are agreed with the Sales Mangers each year.	Number of machines sold by Unit. Degree of customer satisfaction – monitored by customer questionnaire.
• Targets for each sales person are also agreed annually.	Number of machines sold by individuals.

'What new methods, services, products etc. are you planning to introduce in the near future?'

NEW DEVELOPMENTS

> I recognize that markets and customers are changing. We must change the focus of our activities from selling machines to selling systems and solving customer problems. This requires some retraining of the sales staff.

Step 3: *Now describe your information needs for this task*

'Tom, will you now specify the kinds of information that you need to successfully achieve the key task you have just described in detail.

First read again what you wrote down as the principal objectives, critical success factors and major problems associated with carrying out this key task. What information do you require to carry out this task effectively?'

I REQUIRE THE FOLLOWING INFORMATION:

- **To achieve objectives**
1. Number and names of customers buying from companies other than CCC.
2. Number, characteristics and business needs of new account customers.
3. Customer satisfaction with CCC products and service.
4. Degree of motivation and job satisfaction in my sales unit.

- **To attain critical success factors.**
2., 3. and 4. above
5. Which selling strategy is most effective with each customer.

- **To avoid major problems**
  Information on customer problems including late deliveries.
  Knowledge of when members of group are thinking of leaving.

'Now read again the description of the day-to-day activities, problem areas, coordination needs, controls and new developments associated with your most important key task. Write the information you need in the box below.'

I REQUIRE THE FOLLOWING INFORMATION

- **For day-to-day activities**
1. Information on where my salespeople are and the customers they are working with.
2. Information on any problems they are experiencing.
3. Information on the training programmes they are taking.

- **For problems associated with this key task**
4. Any late deliveries of machines to customers.
5. Any problems associated with CAS.
6. Problems due to missing or inaccurate information from Head Office.

- **Coordination problems**
  Due to 4., 5., or 6. above

- **For controls to monitor performance**
7. As a unit are we on course to achieve sales targets?
8. Are individual salespeople meeting their targets?

- **For new developments**
9. Information on how our markets are changing, what customers want to purchase and the kind of service they require.

(Tom would continue examining his other key tasks. These will be omitted for reasons of space.)

Analysis of essential information needs

Step 4: *Specifying essential information needs*

Now read through again your work role information needs and the information needs that you require to complete your most important task effectively. Prioritize these by grading them **E** for essential and **D** for desirable. Separate them into quantitative and qualitative by placing a **Q** beside those which are quantitative. Write your **essential** needs in the box below.

ESSENTIAL INFORMATION NEEDS (E's)

Information for total work role (Mission, critical success factors, major problems)

Quantitative
1. Information on all the projects that my sales group is working on and forecasts of what they are likely to sell.
2. Information on sales targets and progress in meeting these.
3. Information on whether delivery dates are being kept.
4. Information on configuring errors.

Qualitative
5. Information on the skills and knowledge of individual members of my sales group.
6. Information on the state of customer relationships.

ESSENTIAL INFORMATION NEEDS (E's)

> **Key task information – Achieving Sales Targets**
> **(Objectives, critical success factors, major problems)**
> *Quantitative*
> 1. Information on all the projects my sales group is working on and forecasts of what they are likely to sell.
> 2. Information on sales targets and progress in meeting these.
> 3. Information on whether delivery dates are being kept.
> 4. Information on configuring errors.
>
> *Qualitative*
> 5. Information on customer characteristics and business needs.
> 6. Information on state of customer relationships.
> 7. Information on morale and motivation in sales unit.
>
> **Key task information – Achieving Sales Targets**
> **(day-to-day activities, other problems, coordination, controls, new developments)**
> *Quantitative*
> 1. Information on selling success of individual salespeople in Unit.
> 2. Number of configuring errors made by individuals.
>
> *Qualitative*
> 3. Administrative problems with CAS.
> 4. Missing information that is important to selling, e.g. prices and new products.

DESIRABLE INFORMATION (D's)

> **For work role and key task – Achieving Sales Targets**
> *Quantitative*
> 1. Types and numbers of firms buying from companies other than CCC.
>
> *Qualitative*
> 2. Knowledge of resources available to group.
> 3. Which selling strategies are proving most effective.
> 4. Information on how markets are changing.
> 5. Information on CCC business strategies.
> 6. When sales staff are thinking of leaving.

'Tom, you have now thought about and written down your essential and desirable information needs for your higher level work role needs (mission, key tasks, critical success factors and major problems) and for your most important key task.'

Step 5: *Assembling the information model*

You will next work with the rest of the design group assembling the core information model. This requires you to bring together all the essential information needs from each role and function in the Manchester Sales Office. These will be your own information needs and those of the Sales Manager, Richard Keen; the Sales Executive, Jean Harding; the CAS manager, Tony Smith and, if possible, a customer, Ronald Roberts. You will first discuss and agree the higher level information needs related to the Sales Office's mission, key tasks, critical success factors and major problems. Next, following the Beer Viable System Model, for each key task, you will discuss and agree the 'essential' information required to manage day-to-day activities, to reduce and avoid problems and to achieve critical success factors.

As many computer-based information systems can deal more easily with quantitative than qualitative data, it will be useful to split the group's information needs into these two categories.

With most information systems it helps to start small and build up on the basis of use and experience.

Final thoughts

Implementation

The best system is not going to work well unless it is successfully implemented, and many good systems encounter problems at the implementation stage. You need to think carefully about the following.

1. The kinds of problems are likely to be encountered on implementation and how these can be avoided.

2. The activities will have to be coordinated during the implementation period.

3. The amount of time that will be required for implementation, how this should be phased and organized, and how progress can best be monitored.

Evaluation

Once the new system is in and working and has settled down, its ability to contribute to the efficiency, effectiveness and job satisfaction of staff must be evaluated.

Look again at your work mission, key tasks, critical success factors and major problems. Are you now achieving the first three without difficulty while removing or reducing the fourth, and is the new system making a major contribution to this improvement? Look also at your essential information requirements. Is better information making a major contribution to the improvement?

Once the system is in place and working, you should consider future developments. Is your work mission the right one, or should you be changing it to one that is more ambitious? What other new systems would you like to introduce? How can you keep in touch with new organizational and technical developments? Should you be considering further reorganization and innovation? These are all important questions for you and your colleagues.

These appendices are intended to help the reader translate a desire for ethical change into viable action programmes. There are, of course, many ways of doing this, but we all work best when associated with simple tools, a structured approach and a set of clear objectives.

Index

longwall mining 66, 67
Lovelace, Lady 5
Lyons, J. 6

McCarthy, Lord 39
McGregor, D. 53, 54
McNamara, R.S. 8

managers 46
  reflective 44
Manchester University 6
manufacturing processes 2
Marcuse, H. 80
Marx, K. 3
Mayo, E. 53
mechanistic viewpoints 30
memes 18
Metcalf, D.H. 47, 48
methodologies 11, 84
  of systems 11
methods 11
Mill, J.S. 16, 17 60
Miller, A. 9
Miller, E. 68
Montesquieu 16
moral leaders 21
morality 42
motivation 39

National Institute of Industrial Psychology 47
Newnham College 46
Nissan Corporation 35
Norwegian
  democracy experiments 69, 70, 74
Institute of Social research 69
  participation project 69
  printing industry 75

objectives
  definition of 8
office technology 6-8
office work
  feminization of 6
organismic perspective 30
open systems 9
operational research 9
operations analysis 8
organization
  social 18, 19

organizational perspectives 30, 31
  factors 11

Parsons, T.2
participation 39, 44, 56, 57, 83, 84, 86-90, 93, 94-96
Pascal, B. 5
pattern variables 26
People First 37-44
personnel managers 37
Peters, T. 42
philosophers 15-7
philosophy 15, 19
pluralism 52
Plato 15, 16
political science 46, 47
power 49, 50, 52, 58, 60, 61, 103, 104
PPBS (Planned, Programmed Budgeting Systems) 8
Prahalad, C.H. 37
problem solving
  joint 58
Protestant ethic 31, 32

quality of working life 31
QUICKethics 155-64

Rand Corporation 8, 9
rationalisation 3, 34
rationalism 2
Rawls, John 21, 24
redundancies 32, 33, 34
repetitive work 7, 8
Rice, K. 67, 68, 69
Royal Society 5
repetitive strain injury 8
Rousseau, J-J. 16
Rolls-Royce Aerospace 88, 89
Rowntree lecture conferences 47
Royal Astronomical Society 5

Sackman, H. 7
Scheutz, G. 5
Schmidt, Herr 4
Schumacher, E.F. 12
scientific management 3, 4
scientists 20
Smith, A. 1, 2
social
  cohesion 25